Around the World in Eighty Wines

Around the World in Eighty Wines

Exploring Wine
One Country at a Time

MIKE VESETH

ROWMAN & LITTLEFIELD
Lanham • Boulder • New York • London

Published by Rowman & Littlefield
A wholly owned subsidary of The Rowman & Littlefield Publishing Group, Inc.
4501 Forbes Boulevard, Suite 200, Lanham, Maryland 20706
www.rowman.com

Unit A, Whitacre Mews, 26-34 Stannary Street, London SE11 4AB, United Kingdom

Distributed by NATIONAL BOOK NETWORK

British Library Cataloguing in Publication Information Available

Library of Congress Cataloging-in-Publication Data

Names: Veseth, Michael, author.
Title: Around the world in eighty wines : exploring wine one country at a
    time / Mike Veseth.
Description: Lanham, Maryland : Rowman & Littlefield, [2017] | Includes
    bibliographical references and index.
Identifiers: LCCN 2017017271 (print) | LCCN 2017021538 (ebook) | ISBN
    9781442257375 (electronic) | ISBN 9781442257368 (cloth : alk. paper)
Subjects: LCSH: Wine and wine making. | Wineries. | International travel.
Classification: LCC TP548 (ebook) | LCC TP548 .V459 2017 (print) | DDC
    663/.2—dc23
LC record available at https://lccn.loc.gov/2017017271

∞™ The paper used in this publication meets the minimum requirements of
American National Standard for Information Sciences—Permanence of Paper for
Printed Library Materials, ANSI/NISO Z39.48-1992.

Printed in the United States of America

Contents

Part IV: Sour Grapes?

Part I

FROM LONDON
TO BEIRUT

Chapter 1

London

The Challenge Is Made and the Journey Begins

The Reform Club is an imposing stone structure that is warmer and more ornate inside than out. If you have visited London you may have walked right past it without appreciating its significance. It sits serenely, surrounded by other imposing buildings, on Pall Mall, just down the road from Charing Cross tube station and Trafalgar Square in the midst of what is sometimes called London's clubland. The architecture bears a distinct resemblance to Michelangelo's Palazzo Farnese in Rome, according to club documents, and on close inspection the similarities are clear even to an untrained eye.

The Reform Club was founded in 1836 as an opposing force to the Tory Club and the palatial clubhouse building opened in 1841.[1] Membership was originally limited to those who had supported the Reform Act of 1832, hence the name. The grand palace became for a time the de facto headquarters of the Liberal Party although today there is no particular political affiliation associated with the organization. You can tour the place if you like, providing you appear on a particular Saturday in September having previously made application to the General Office. It's a private club, you see.

The reason that you may remember the name of the Reform Club, even if you are not an authority on Victorian political movements and even if you are not well acquainted with Italian Renaissance architecture, is that it was here, on Tuesday, October 1, 1872, that club member Phileas Fogg accepted a wager from a fellow "Reformer" that would change his life. You are familiar with the story if you have read Jules Verne's account of the adventure that followed. Its title is *Around the World in Eighty Days.*

It is a short walk from the Reform Club on Pall Mall to Berry Bros. & Rudd at 3 St. James's Street, just down the road and to the right. You can walk there in six minutes, according to Google Maps, or maybe a little less time if you are in a hurry, as Phileas Fogg might have been. There's no record to indicate that Fogg stopped at Berry Bros. on that famous day in October, or any other day for that matter, but the shop in the plain, dark-red brick building with the ornate arched windows was certainly open that day, having done business there since its founding in 1698 by the Widow Bourne. George Berry came to work there in 1801 and his name went up on the sign above the door in 1810. Two of his sons, George Jr. and Henry, started running the establishment together in 1845, welcoming any and all to their premises. It's a wine shop, you see, although they traded in coffee and other commodities in earlier years, and is as open to the public as the Reform Club seems to be closed. It is the location I have chosen to begin the adventure that fills this book, which I call *Around the World in Eighty Wines.*

CENTER OF THE WORLD?

Why start here, in London, apart from a perhaps misguided desire to create parallels with Jules Verne's famous story? Well, London was the center of Verne's world in a certain way because it was the control center of the "sun never sets upon" British Empire, which in 1872 really did span the globe. The center of the world? Well, if you had to pick one place you could have done worse than London, which is one reason Verne located his hero here.

It might surprise you to know that for much of history London has also been the center of the world of wine. Not the production of wine. You won't see many vines on your scenic Thames River cruise, although British vineyards today produce wines, especially sparklers, of rising reputation. No, it's the wine trade that is centered here, and because of that, wine critics, wine writers, and wine educators are disproportionately drawn to London as well. It started, to pick a date, in the cathedral in Poitiers on Whitsunday (May 18) of 1152 when the future King Henry II married Eleanor of Aquitaine. By this act a vast swath of southwest France came under British control, including an area that we will visit in the next chapter, Bordeaux. For the next three hundred years the vines of Bordeaux were Britain's vineyards. British investment in the French wine industry and British consumption of vast quantities of the stuff led inevitably to a sophisticated wine trade that continues to this day.[2]

Jules Verne reports that Phileas Fogg took good advantage of London's central place in the world of wine at the Reform Club, where he had breakfast and dinner each and every day. "Club decanters, of a lost mold," Verne tells us, "contained his sherry, his port, and his cinnamon-spiced claret; while his beverages were refreshingly cooled with ice, brought at great cost from the American lakes."[3] Sherry, port, and claret, the traditional British name for the wines of Bordeaux. Nothing could be more logical for the refined Mr. Fogg. And no better place to begin our journey, I think, than 3 St. James's Street and the Berry Bros. & Rudd doorway.[4]

THE CHALLENGE

The challenge for Phileas Fogg was relatively straightforward. A story in the *Daily Telegraph* pronounced that, using scheduled commercial steamship and rail transport links, it would be possible to circle the globe in eighty days, which represented a tremendous triumph of technology and rational calculation over nature and distance. This journey was an audacious idea in the Victorian age and not an easy thing to accomplish even today using boats, trains, and so on. BBC television presenter Michael Palin struggled to match Fogg's pace on the same basic route in his 1989 television series, even using modern fast trains and ships. Cheating—which in this case means taking to the air—makes the task almost ridiculously easy.[5] The supersonic Concorde holds the record for a full circumnavigation by a commercial jetliner following the equator, more or less—just under thirty-two hours. Wow!

Eighty days? Nonsense, the members of the Reform Club who were gathered around declared. Not nonsense, Fogg replied, and he bet twenty thousand British pounds that he could do it, starting at once. This was a very bold thing to do, not just because the idea came out of the blue, but because one pound in 1872 had the purchasing power of about eighty pounds today, therefore making the wager the equivalent of £1.6 million or about $2 million. What nerves the cool, rational Mr. Fogg must have had to make such a bet and what trust he must have had in reason and technology. Although I am a trained economist and schooled in the ways of rational thought, I would not have made Phileas Fogg's bet, not for $2 million or $20 million or any sum at all.

The challenge I set, and the figurative wager I make with you, the reader, is much different. I propose to lead you on a journey around the world collecting eighty precious bottles to try to answer a simple question. Why wine?

Why wine? What kind of question is that? Well, you know what I mean. What is it about wine that captures our imagination today much as it must have done eight thousand years ago? Why has wine inspired our passions over the centuries and around the globe? What is wine's hold on us and why does it endure? Why—to get personal for a moment—are you so interested in wine that you have this book in your hands when there are thousands of other books on other topics that you could be reading instead? There must be something very special about wine—something beyond acid, sugar, alcohol, and the other constituent parts. Why wine? It's a good question and I am willing to go to some trouble to try to find the answer.

Answering this question in our Phileas Fogg way will require us to collect a big case of wine, but it is really stories that we are after. Every glass of wine tells a story and so each of our eighty wines must tell an important tale. And then—this is the really hard part—the various wines that we choose must not just each tell their own story. They must be like the tiles of a mosaic or the colored-paint points of a Georges Seurat painting—they must collectively form a picture and tell a story that reveals a greater truth.

A greater truth? About what? About wine? About the world? Don't ask me—seriously I am not the right one to ask. Sitting here at the start of our journey, I know that the greater truth must exist and I believe in my heart that wine can reveal it. But I don't know what it will be. Like you, I am here for the journey and I hope that my wishes will come true.

What will the eighty wines reveal? Come with me on this journey and we will find out together!

I take inspiration from many sources in this quest, Jules Verne's novel most of all because of the author's cleverly hidden agenda. While the account of Fogg's journey appears to be about the mechanics of travel over great distance, the story itself goes much deeper, which accounts for its incredible staying power. Distance is not really the enemy, you see, it is human nature, and Fogg achieves his goal (and wins his bet) not through technological advance and rational calculation as he imagined at the start, but through the admirable human qualities of courage, strength, loyalty, and love, with Fogg and his companion Passepartout as the unexpected heroes. It is the race against time that draws us to *Around the World in Eighty Days*, but it is the human drama (and what the journey reveals about them and us) that makes this tale so memorable. I hope our journey through the world of wine will trace a similar path.

Jules Verne taught me that journeys don't reveal their significance all at once or in carefully measured doses. They ebb and flow like life itself. These deeper currents are what I hope to explore in this book, with wine rather than boats, trains, and elephants as our mode of transport. But let me assure you that I will never forget that the reason you picked up this book in the first place was a fascination with wine or travel or both, because I share that fascination with you.

THE ROAD AHEAD

So where are we going on this quest to find eighty wines that capture the essence of what wine is all about and why it is so important? Well, here is the plan, although I warn you that there might be some unexpected detours along the way (like Phileas Fogg and Passepartout, you will need to roll with the punches).

We start in London for the reasons you have just read and then our next steps are very logical, quite as if Phileas Fogg had made the plan for us. We jump the channel to France and learn that, while you should not judge a book by its cover, people judge French wines by the shape of their bottles all the time. Then on to Italy to prove the impossibility of Italian wine. We continue to Syria, Georgia, and Lebanon (not so far from Cairo, which was Fogg's next stop) where wine and war are the concerns, although maybe not the kind of war you expect.

We will catch up with Fogg in India eventually, but not before we add more bottles to our traveling wine cellar. Part Two of the book circles back through North Africa from Beirut to Spain. Then begins a long journey that follows the Portuguese trade routes of earlier times, from rainy Porto and its namesake fortified wine to the hot island of Madeira and then on to the Cape Winelands at the tip of Africa. We round the Cape and arrive in India via a fascinating but most indirect route: Cape Town to Bali to Bangkok and finally Mumbai, with wine at every stop. I think you will enjoy the ride!

Part Three climbs high in the mountains where China meets Tibet at a place called Shangri-La. Wine in China? Shangri-La? Lots for us to explore here. Then we jet off to Australia to engage in a rather heated debate about wine's soul. Tasmania is the next stop, where we discover that it is hot to be cool. The Southern Cross guides us to New Zealand, Chile, and Argentina, three very different countries that are united in an unexpected way by their relationship to wine.

The final leg of the journey takes us north and then east across the continent and then the Atlantic Ocean to our London finish line. Along the way we take the wine train to Napa Valley, stop in Seattle for a Riesling Rendezvous, and make a Cannonball Run across North America, ending up at an Italian restaurant in Thomas Jefferson's Virginia. Then it's a short hop to London and time for a final accounting. Did we make it? Will our eighty wines pass the test? You will be asked to judge if the challenge has been met.

I can't guarantee that we will succeed in our quest, but I'll bet you won't be bored with the journey. Please heed this warning: There are lots of wines, lots of stories, and we can only choose eighty of them here, so I am going to have to be incredibly selective and my choices won't always agree with yours. This will drive you nuts (it would drive me nuts), but I promise there is method in my madness and that I will make it up to you at the end of the trip. If this were easy and the choices obvious, why would we bother?

It's an ambitious itinerary—maybe even a crazy one! Turn the page and begin it with me.

But before we go, let's take time to taste our first wine. Well begun is half done, they say, so let me choose a special edition of Winston Churchill's favorite wine, Champagne Pol Roger, and raise a toast to the journey ahead. To love, life, health, and eighty bottles of wine. Cheers!

～

The Wine

Champagne Pol Roger Cuvée Winston Churchill, Champagne, France

～

Chapter 2

France

Which Bottle? Which Wine?

Phileas Fogg left London for France and beyond, but he didn't pause on his way south and east. No time for vineyards and wineries or long philosophical lunches with many corks pulled and bottles drained. Too bad for him! Our purpose is different and so a more extended stay in France is unavoidable. They say that you can't tell a book by its cover, but we have come to France to learn why sometimes you can tell a wine by its bottle, because France, the people of France, and the world of wine are divided over two kinds of bottles.[1] This is a tale of two wine bottles, the wines inside them, the forces that have shaped both the wines and the bottles, and the competing ideas of wine that they represent. In other words, this is the story of Burgundy and Bordeaux.

WHICH WINE BOTTLE?

Wine from Bordeaux, which is located on the southwest coast of France, comes in a bottle that always reminds me of a soldier standing ramrod straight at attention. If you've ever seen the changing of the guard at Buckingham Palace, you know what I mean. The sides are straight and parallel, the shoulders high, and the short neck pronounced. It is so different from a Burgundy bottle, which strikes me as much more feminine, graceful, sensual, its sides curving seductively with soft shoulders and an elegant long neck. Am I romanticizing the wine bottles and perhaps also the wines? If so, I am not alone. Some experts say that Bordeaux's best wines are experienced from the neck up—they need disciplined appreciation—while those from Burgundy are sensuously felt down below in the region where emotions rule.[2] Head and heart. If this is true (obviously you should pull some corks and see what you think and feel) then the impressions given by the bottle shapes and my romantic descriptions of them do not lie.

Burgundy and Bordeaux wines did not always come in these particular types of bottles. Indeed, for hundreds of years they did not come in bottles at all. Early wine bottles were too delicate and expensive; a common bottle shape was more like an onion than either a member of the Queen's Guard or a beautiful woman. Glass was blown into a roundish mold because the more spherical shape holds larger volumes per unit of glass, and glass and glass blowing did not come cheap. The resulting bottles could only be stored upright and were easily broken; and corks could easily dry out if the wine was held for very long, letting in oxygen and spoiling the wine inside.

For this reason as your ship sailed down the Gironde River from Bordeaux out into the Atlantic, the wine in the hold destined for London (and perhaps for Berry Bros. & Rudd) was in casks or barrels and would be delivered in this way to taverns and shops that dispensed the wine into glasses, jugs, and bottles for final sale. Barrels and casks were a practical solution to the problem of shipping wine, much as the huge container-filling twenty-four-thousand-liter wine bladders that facilitate the global bulk wine trade solve that problem today.[3] But there were problems, too. Barrels are never completely airtight and so you need to continually top them up or the oxygen would cause the wine to spoil. And of course the wine producer loses control when wine is shipped in this way, as consumers are likely to associate wine quality with the seller rather than the often-anonymous maker.

The modern wine bottle was born at the end of the seventeenth century when British glassmakers found a way to make bottles stronger than before—strong enough, in fact, to safely contain sparkling wine, thus solving the problem of Champagne, which is fermented in the bottle and previously had suffered from the inconvenient tendency of bottles to spontaneously explode from the pressure within. The new Champagne bottles' stronger glass and deep punt provided security for the precious bubbles within. Burgundy, Champagne's near neighbor, adopted a version of that bottle as its own, but the bottle the Bordelais eventually perfected had a different shape.

Partly this was because the Queen's Guard bottle stacks better on its side, which is very useful if you are "laying down" wine to age, as is often done with Bordeaux wines (this keeps the cork damp too, preserving the wine) and I suspect that the compact cylindrical shape was also useful in shipping the wines because they fit efficiently into crates. Bordeaux wine, after all, had to get across the sea to its main market in London in good shape, whereas Burgundy traveled a much shorter distance by river, canal, or wagon to Paris and Lyon. There was a lot of Bordeaux to move because the Bordeaux vineyards were and are vast. Burgundy, spread out in thin ribbons following the River Saône, is a very much smaller region with tiny total output compared with Bordeaux.

So which is for you—the masculine Bordeaux bottle or the more feminine shape from Burgundy? Is it purely a matter of taste? Does the question even matter? Well, I think it does because these bottles are symbolic of not just the wine in them and the regions they represent but also of France itself. And of two competing ideas of both France and wine.

TWO IDEAS OF WINE

The contrasts begin with what's in the bottle. Burgundy's best-known red wines are pure Pinot Noir, a temperamental grape variety that likes a cooler climate, which Burgundy generously provides. Maybe a bit too cool in some years and rainy, too. Pinot lives its life on the edge and making great wines is a constant challenge.

The most famous red Bordeaux wines, on the other hand, are made from Cabernet Sauvignon, Merlot, Cabernet Franc, Malbec, and Petit Verdot, which are much more tannic grape varieties than Pinot Noir (hence the desire for bottle aging) that love the sun and are grown with some success in almost every wine region around the world. The Bordeaux vineyards are as broad and abundant as the river-hugging Burgundy ones are narrow and spare. Bordeaux is big because its mission in life is to fill a huge export pipeline to Great Britain, Northern Europe, and beyond. Burgundy couldn't begin to satisfy a thirst like that—just not enough land, grapes, and wine. Burgundy isn't for the world, it is for France and for the elites of Paris in particular. Indeed, according to Jean-Robert Pitte, the critical moment in Burgundian wine history occurred in 1694 when King Louis XIV's physician, Fagon, determined that the king's gout was being exacerbated by constant consumption of his favorite still wines from the Champagne region. Fagon persuaded him to substitute soft, pure, aged Burgundy for the more acidic Champagne wines, thus creating a fashion for Burgundy at Versailles and in Paris and a market for these wines as well.[4] Champagne's lost royal market was eventually recovered when it was discovered that those acidic still wines were much improved by a secondary bubble-forming bottle fermentation. Pop! Sparkling Champagne was born!

MONEY AND RELIGION

The list of differences between Burgundy and Bordeaux goes on and on but it is impossible to ignore the most basic one. In many ways Bordeaux represents wine as a business opportunity while Burgundy channels wine's mystical, almost religious side.

Business came naturally to Bordeaux from the early days of exports to England, but the critical moment was when the Classification of 1855 appeared. Asked to rank the wines of Bordeaux for an exhibit at the international fair in Paris, the charged group of wine merchants based the rankings on the most objective measure they knew. Not "reputation," whatever that means, and not blind tasting either. No, they simply looked up the wholesale prices of the wines. Four of them earned prices consistently above the rest and were placed in the top tier. Château Margaux, Château Latour, Château Lafite, Château Haut-Brion—you probably recognize the names—were the first growths then and the first growths now. It took decades for the 1855 runner-up—now called Château Mouton Rothschild—to be elevated to the highest status. Second growths, third growths, and so on down the line, all the important Bordeaux estates were ranked, creating a hierarchy and an ordered set of powerful wine brands. Much has changed in Bordeaux over the years and wines in the lower ranks have risen and fallen, but money talks and the wines at the top have remained an unlikely constant despite changes in wines, vines, vineyards, styles, and weather.[5]

The idea of Bordeaux is dominated by the châteaux, the producers. Burgundy has its equivalent concept in the domaine, and although the advice for those who want to taste the great Burgundy wines is still to choose a good producer, choose a good vintage (because the weather is so variable), and then choose the wine, the dominant belief by far is *terroir*, or sense of place. Vineyards are rated in Burgundy, not producers, and many famous Grand Cru or Premier Cru vineyards, tiny as they are, provide grapes for dozens of different producers all eager to make wine from the finest fruit. Thus a wine made by Henri Jayer, a famous producer, is a treat, and to have a wine made with grapes from the Richebourg Grand Cru vineyard on the Côte de Nuits is a fantastic experience. To have them both together, to taste a Henri Jayer Richebourg Grand Cru, well, it is as good as it gets. Or at least it is just about the most expensive thing that can be done in wine, according to a 2015 article in *Decanter* magazine, which cited an average price of more than fifteen thousand dollars per bottle.[6]

It is not too extreme and only a little sacrilegious to say that Burgundy lovers worship the ground the *vignerons* walk on—vineyards—and study the maps and the fine lines that divide the vines as if it were a religious text. One famous Grand Cru vineyard—Domaine de la Romanée Conti—even has a cross in the vineyard, and another Grand Cru vineyard, Clos de Vougeot, was in fact established by Cistercian monks of Cîteaux Abbey, and it is here that wine in Burgundy was nurtured and preserved in the Middle Ages. Is Burgundy a religion? Pretty close if you ask me.

The 1,247 individual designated plots (called *climats*) of the Côte de Beaune and Côte de Nuits came one step closer to sainthood in 2015 when they were designated a UNESCO World Heritage Site (joining Champagne and about twenty other similarly recognized wine regions). "The UNESCO designation gives a global imprimatur to the French view that great wine can be produced only through a magical combination of climate, geography, and history—that ineffable quality often called 'terroir,'" according to a *New York Times* report.[7] French idea, maybe, but Burgundian gospel for sure.

If you think of French wine as rugged *vignerons* struggling against bad weather and harsh market forces on a tiny plot of land to make wine that is pure, natural, and authentic, then you are Burgundian at heart and you must drink the fine wines of this region. Not all the wines from Burgundy are like this—indeed probably most of them are not if you look at the numbers—but that's the idea that is cultivated here. It is one side of French wine and of France, too. If, on the other hand, you see the market for wine as the friendly ghost that delivers the world to your doorstep and you appreciate the ratings that guide your selection and the security that famous brands provide, then you lean to the side of Bordeaux in this battle.

So how do you think of wine? Winemaker or *terroir*? Commerce or philosophy? Business or religion? The lines are drawn and wine lovers are sometimes forced to choose between two ideas of French wine, of France itself, and of the world, too, I suppose.

WHICH TWO BOTTLES?

The time has come to start to fill the remaining seventy-nine spots in our global wine collection, and you can see why representatives of Burgundy and Bordeaux must be included in our global cellar. But which ones? To lovers of Burgundy and Bordeaux the particular choice matters a great deal and would be the source of a nearly endless debate. Lafite or Margaux (and which vintage)? Henri Jayer or Domaine de la Romanée Conti? I admit to having personal favorites, but the choice is as much about people as the wines themselves. For Burgundy I will always remember a bottle of Maison Joseph Drouhin Chambolle-Musigny Amoureuses (the lovers—it's the name of the vineyard) that my wife Sue and I shared on our wedding anniversary a few years ago.

For Bordeaux it has to be a double magnum (three liters, equivalent to four bottles) of Château Petrus 1994 that was served by a close friend at a dinner to celebrate his son's (and my student's) university graduation. The big empty bottle is displayed (much to Sue's annoyance) on our living room hearth. Burgundy and Bordeaux, heart and head, wedding anniversary and university graduation. I can't think of better bottles to begin our collection, can you? But I must admit that these wines mean so much to me because of the memories they spark about these particular occasions and the special people I shared them with. That's what wine does and why we love it so.

Burgundy and Bordeaux make some of the most famous (and most expensive) wines in the world.[8] But both regions have a secret. The top wines are just the tip of an iceberg. Down below and out of sight are much larger quantities of lesser wines that must somehow be sold to pay the bills. They stand on the reputations of the top wines in one way or another, but Château Cash Flow is what they are really all about. I call them Black Friday wines.

BLACK FRIDAY WINES: A TALE OF TWO HOLIDAYS

Although the United States is not the only country to set aside a day for giving thanks, we like to think of Thanksgiving as our distinctive holiday. It was conceived as a day for deep reflection, but Thanksgiving has evolved into a long weekend of overconsumption and discount shopping. Some of my friends really prefer to celebrate Black Friday, the day after Thanksgiving, when the holiday shopping season formally begins and retailers find out if they will be "in the black" for the year based upon early sales data.

Black Friday wines are wines made specifically for the purpose of turning a profit. Nothing wrong in that since wineries need to make money to stay in business, but sometimes they free-ride on the reputations of others or rely on slick marketing rather than great winemaking to do so (much as the Black Friday holiday was created purely for commercial purposes). Both Burgundy and Bordeaux have their share of Black Friday wines. They have to in order to support their wine industries. I wrote about one of Bordeaux's Black Friday wines in my 2013 book *Extreme Wine*.[9] It is called Mouton Cadet and it is one of the most widely distributed wines in the world. It is made by the same company that produces the first growth Château Mouton Rothschild, but the grapes are sourced from throughout the Bordeaux region, not from the winery estate, and millions of bottles are produced each year. It is a nice wine, don't get me wrong, and stands high above many other Black Friday Bordeaux wines that are hard to sell even at low prices. I use it only as an example of a wine produced in large quantities and riding just a bit on the reputation of its more illustrious relation.

Burgundy has its share of similar wines, made with regional rather than vineyard designation. Some are better than others, but they all need to be sold somehow to pay the bills. My favorite Black Friday Burgundy, however, actually comes from Beaujolais, the part of the region to the south where the red wines are made from Gamay Noir, not Pinot Noir. The difference in grape varieties and winemaking methods is enough that many people don't realize the Beaujolais is part of Burgundy.[10] The difference is magnified when it comes to Beaujolais Nouveau.

Beaujolais Nouveau is not an especially thoughtful wine or a tenderly sensuous one, either. If wine were literature, my friend Patrick points out,

Nouveau would be the trashy paperback novel you read at the beach. Nothing wrong in that—everyone needs an escape once in a while. The grapes for Nouveau are picked in late September or thereabouts and the only thing that prevents instant sale is the necessity of fermentation and the mechanics of distribution. It's still a bit sweet when it's bottled and sometimes a little fizzy, too, when it arrives with great fanfare on the third Thursday in November (a week before Turkey Day in the United States). Best served cold (like revenge!) it is perhaps the ultimate cash flow wine.

Nouveau is not very sophisticated, so why do the French, who otherwise are known to guard their *terroirist* image, bother with it? The Beaujolais producers make very nice Cru Beaujolais (non-nouveau) wines; character, complexity, you can have it all and for a surprisingly low price. Ah, but that's the problem. Sitting close to prestigious Burgundy, the Beaujolais cannot command high prices for their wines, good as they are, so they must try to make money through turnover more than markup. They churn out millions of bottles of Nouveau to pay the bills.

At the peak of the bubble in 1992 about half of all wines made in Beaujolais were Nouveau. The proportion remains high even today. Ironically, Nouveau often sells at prices as high as Beaujolais' more serious wines because it is marketed so well. So it is hard to see why you'd want to buy it instead of the region's other wines. It's easy, on the other hand, to see why you'd want to sell it. If the makers can sell their Nouveau, then maybe the bottom line for the year will be in the black. If the Nouveau market fails, well that red stain on the floor won't be just spilled wine.

Nouveau is therefore generally marketed around the world with more than the usual urgency (just as those Black Friday retail store sales seem a little desperate at times)—and not just because young wines hit their "best by" date pretty quickly. Nouveau is usually distributed around the world via expensive air freight rather than more economic sea transport in part because the short time between harvest and final sale makes speed a factor, although some considerations have been made in recent years to mitigate accusations of the wine's big carbon footprint.

Sweet, fizzy, and at one point sold in lightweight PET bottles—Beaujolais Nouveau sounds like the perfect wine for American consumers brought up on two-liter jugs of fizzy-sweet Mountain Dew and Diet Coke. If you were cynical, you would think Nouveau was an American wine . . . made in the USA.

And it is, in a way. Although the wine obviously comes from France (and there is actually a long tradition of simple and fun early-release new wines in France and elsewhere), I think it is fair to say that the Nouveau *phenomenon* is an American invention.

W.J. Deutsch & Sons, the American distributors, really put Beaujolais in general and Nouveau in particular on the U.S. wine-market map when they became exclusive distributors for Georges Duboeuf some years ago. They took this simple wine and made it a marketing event. To paraphrase an old Vulcan proverb, only Nixon could go to China and only the brilliant Deutsch family firm could sell Nouveau! In fact they were so successful that they partnered with another family firm—the Casella family from Australia—and created a second wine phenomenon tailored to American tastes: Yellow Tail!

So let me add Mouton Cadet and Duboeuf Beaujolais Nouveau to the circumnavigation wine collection to show that there are more than two sides to French wine. Yes, there are Burgundy and Bordeaux but they come in both noble and humble variants. But enough! We must pack up our wines and head for the next stop on our (and Phileas Fogg's) itinerary. On to Italy!

I know what you are saying! How can you leave France without visiting other regions including the Rhône, Champagne, Alsace, the Loire . . . the list goes on and on. And what about the white wines (Chablis!) and the sweet wines (Sauternes!)? Yes, these wines are worthy, too, but that eighty wine bet limits me in the same way the eighty days constrained Phileas Fogg. So if I have already ignored your favorite wine, let me say this. Trust me. I'll make it up to you somewhere along the way. If I don't, then I guess all bets are off!

⌒

The Wines
Chateau Petrus 1994, Bordeaux, France

Maison Joseph Drouhin Chambolle-Musigny Amoreuses, Burgundy, France

Mouton Cadet Rouge, Bordeaux, France

Georges Duboeuf Beaujolais Nouveau, Beaujolais, France

⌒

Chapter 3

Italy

Batali's Impossibility Theorem

If Phileas Fogg stopped for even a moment in Italy to savor the wine, sip an espresso, or munch on a bit of cheese, we know nothing about it from the Jules Verne book. In fact, we know nothing of the journey from the moment he left Charing Cross station in London until his arrival on the docks in Brindisi except that he changed trains in Paris, then on to Turin via Mont Cenis and on down Italy's boot to the heel. Perhaps he never looked up from his timetables, atlases, and maps as his train sped toward Brindisi, where he would catch the Peninsular and Oriental Company freighter *Mongolia*. His was a race against time. Unlike Fogg, Italy is impossible for *us* to overlook, but we need to try to see and understand it in the right way, which is more complicated than you might think.

The principle that I like to call "Batali's Impossibility Theorem" is named after Mario Batali, the American chef and restaurateur who has done so much to promote all things Italian here in the United States.[1] Americans sometimes talk about "Italian food," which we love, and the "Italian restaurants" that serve it, but Batali has said that there is no such thing as Italian food—there are only the many regional cuisines of Italy and these can't and shouldn't be reduced to a single generic category. Anyone who has traveled to or lived in Italy knows that he is right about this. Tuscan, Roman, and Neapolitan cuisine are different and distinct, influenced as they are by different ingredients and traditions, and this is just scratching the surface.

Stated more generally, Batali's Theorem is that complicated things are best understood and appreciated in complicated ways—by explicitly considering their many sides rather than trying to reduce them to a generalization that conceals far more than it reveals. Batali's Theorem seems especially relevant in today's smartphone-equipped, web-enabled world where anyone with the least interest can drill down through the surface layer of any question to find a treasure trove of tasty detail. Batali's Theorem isn't an abstract concept; it is something that seems to guide us every day.

THE IMPOSSIBILITY OF ITALIAN WINE

What is Italian wine? Everything and nothing—it's impossible to define, which is the point. Is it red or white (or maybe rosé)? Sparkling or still? Strong in spirit or low in alcohol? Is it bold and brave or light and delicate? I hope you will agree with me that Italian wine is all of these things and more, which is to say that it is not one particular thing but many things. And I hope you will also agree that Batali's Impossibility Theorem applies here: there is really no such thing as Italian wine, only the regional wines of Italy. And what a world of wines they are!

Ian D'Agata's 2014 book *Native Wine Grapes of Italy* identifies 377 indigenous Italian wine grapes, which is not only a large absolute number of different wine sources, it is also a very significant proportion of all the world's grape varieties.[2] The comprehensive reference *Wine Grapes* by Jancis Robinson, Julia Harding, and José Vouillamoz lists 1,368 wine grape varieties in the entire world, so Italy alone accounts more than a quarter of global wine's potential wine grape diversity. Italian wine grape heritage is as important in its own way as the country's well-recognized contributions to global music, art, architecture, and cuisine.[3] If you add international varieties that are planted in Italian vineyards (Merlot, Cabernet, Chardonnay, Sauvignon Blanc, and so forth) it becomes clear that a rich world of wine awaits the thirsty student of the wines of Italy.

Batali's Theorem applies because although some grape varieties and wine styles span several Italian regions, most are far more local than national or global and reflect a very particular geographic and cultural *terroir*. Having lived in Italy a bit and traveled there quite a lot, I have a few favorites among the hundreds of regional wines. One that I discovered in Bologna is Pignoletto, both still and *frizzante*, a white wine that seems to be the perfect foil for the region's rich cheeses and meats. And I can still taste the Ruché that we found at a regional food festival in Moncalvo, which was being proudly poured by a civic club from Castagnole Monferrato, the grape's historic home base.

My personal list of Italian regional wine discoveries is quite long, but leafing through D'Agata's book makes me thirsty for more. One that I can't wait to sample is Mostosa from Emilia-Romagna, so named it is said because of the large quantities of must (*mosto*) that it produces and the large quantities of wine that result. A productive grape, you might say, and perhaps for that reason it is sometimes associated with a wine known as Pagadebit (debt-payer).

ONE WINE TO RULE THEM ALL?

I suppose Batali's Impossibility Theorem is especially important to me because at one point in planning this book I toyed with the idea that it might be possible to visit different places and select one wine to represent each region. It seemed like a great challenge and for a while I thought I had found my single "Italian" wine. Not Chianti or Brunello, Barolo or Barbaresco. Not Amarone either, as much as I enjoy it. No, my Italian wine candidate came from an unexpected place and a little known grape. Let me tell you about it.

Lots of images come to mind when you think of Venice—the art, the architecture, the canals and gondolas. Vineyards? Not so much. Can't imagine vineyards in Venice, although historians tell us that they were there—some even in the San Marco quarter—in earlier days when the city was less crowded with tourists and more concerned with self-sufficiency.

Would you be surprised if I told you that there are still vines and wines in Venice today? Not on the cluster of islands that we think of as the city of Venice proper, but out in the busy lagoon? You must take the passenger ferry to the island of Burano (the island of lacemakers to distinguish it from Murano, the island of glassmakers) and, connected by a short footbridge, you will find the island of Mazzorbo and the one-hectare vineyard of Venissa, which is planted with Dorona di Venezia, a grape of the Venetian lagoon. Its natural resistance to fungal diseases is a plus in this humid place. Known since the fifteenth century, it is a natural cross of Garganega and Bermestia Bianca (according to my copy of *Wine Grapes*) that is popular as a table grape because of its big sweet golden (*d'oro*) globe fruit. You can find Dorona here and there in the Veneto (easy to mistake it for Garganega, the grape most associated with Soave) but until recently not so much in Venice and its lagoon islands, the challenges of maritime grape-growing being what they are. But Gianluca Bisol, of the famous Prosecco house, discovered a few vines on the island of Sant'Erasmo and used them to establish a Dorona vineyard on the old ScarpaVolo estate property on nearby Mazzorbo.

Golden grape, golden wine. The wine really is golden due in part to fermentation on the grape skins to give it special character. The bottles of hand-crafted glass display rich decorations of hand-beaten gold foil (thus honoring two traditional Venetian crafts). The name Venissa and a number are carefully hand-etched on each bottle.

What does it taste like? Only two vintages had been released at the time of our visit—2010 and 2011—and Ian D'Agata writes that he prefers the freshness of the 2011. Winemakers Desiderio Bisol and Roberto Cipresso apparently pulled back from some of the extreme cellar practices after the first vintage, yielding a fresher wine, although not something that you would ever mistake for Soave! Sue and I loved the color of the wine and were surprised by its delicate aromas. I found a certain saltiness very appealing, although maybe that was the power of suggestion since we were tasting the wine with Matteo Bisol looking out at the vineyard and the lagoon just beyond. If there really is a salty character, the wine comes by it naturally. Saltwater floods the vineyards during periodic tidal surges and a good deal of effort goes into drainage. I preferred the more intense 2010, but maybe that's to be expected of the author of a book called *Extreme Wine*. A red wine made from Merlot and Carmenère grapes raised on another tiny lagoon island was released in 2014. Sue and I noted richness, intensity, and a salty personality.

On the ferry ride back to San Marco with the full moon above us, Sue and I talked about Venissa. I was suspicious at the start that it was a platform to promote the Bisol brand, but my hypothesis didn't hold up. It really seems to be a sincere attempt by the Bisol family to honor the history and traditions of Venice and Venetian wine. What makes Venissa so interesting is that it is a *living* exhibition—the actual vineyards are right here in the lagoon, not just dots on an old map, and the actual wine is in your glass, not just a label on the wall. This obviously creates a more intense sensual experience. And the total project reinforces this by drawing on all the senses through the packaging, the location, the inn and restaurant, and so forth.

I hope you can appreciate that, cruising serenely back to Venice, it was possible to imagine that Venissa was the Special One—the one wine to represent all of Italy because of the statement it makes about culture, history, and wine. But then, inevitably, the force of Batali's Impossibility Theorem made itself apparent. Venissa is full of meaning, but Venissa alone cannot carry the full burden of Italy's diverse wine culture. Every Italian region should have its Venissa (and I think many of them do if you look very closely), but no single wine, not even one as carefully conceived as this one, can possibly do the job. But we don't have room for *every* Italian wine in our eighty-wine case. What now?

UNRAVELLING THE IMPOSSIBLE: HOW MANY WINES?

Tre Bicchieri—three glasses. Those are important words if you are interested in Italian wine. *The Michelin Guide* gives up to three stars to the top restaurants in France and around the world and perhaps for that reason *Gambero Rosso* magazine's *Vini d'Italia* (*Italian Wines* is the title of the English edition) gives up to three glasses to Italy's finest wines.[4] This seems like an objective starting point. How many wines from Italy could there possibly be and how many of them would qualify for the highest award?

My hopes quickly sank when I did the math. For the 2015 edition the editors surveyed 2,042 wineries and evaluated twenty thousand wines (and they were selective—not every wine or winery made the cut). Twenty thousand wines! If you or I were to try to taste that may wines in flights of five different wines each evening it would take almost eleven years to complete the task. And by the time we finished there would be thousands more lined up. The *Gambero Rosso* tasters were very selective as they always are and out of that huge list, just 423 wines (about 2 percent) received the *Tre Bicchieri* rating. Four hundred and twenty-three. That's way too many wines. What next?

As usual, Sue provided the critical insight. The key is to try to think of Italian wine in a different way, she said. The defining characteristic of Italian wines is their diversity, and diversity comes in many forms. If you think of it in terms of diversity of grape varieties and wine styles, then there is almost no end to the wines that should be included. If you think in terms of geographic diversity the same dead end appears. But there are other ways to think about wine.

New York Times columnist Thomas Friedman once defined globalization as "everything and its opposite," which is a more useful characterization than it might seem. Since I've already started my list of wines from Italy with golden Venissa, perhaps it might be interesting to look at the opposite side of the wine coin. Venissa is all about history and luxury and making a personal statement about what Italian wines are meant to be. It is also an example of what I have called elsewhere an "imaginary wine."[5] It isn't truly imaginary—it really exists. Sue and I have even tasted it, but it is produced in such limited quantities and is available in so few places that unless you travel to that island in the Venetian lagoon your chances of enjoying it yourself are almost zero. For all intents and purposes it might as well be fiction, like Phileas Fogg. Alas, wine magazines are full of articles about un-attainable, almost imaginary wines that most of us will never have a chance to experience.

FROM IMAGINARY TO INVISIBLE

The opposite of an imaginary wine like Venissa is a wine that is so ubiquitous that we take it for granted. It is essentially invisible because it is overlooked. With this in mind and at Sue's suggestion, I choose Riunite Lambrusco, a sparkling wine from Emilia-Romagna (Bologna's province), which was for a stunning twenty-six years the best-selling Italian wine in the United States. Indeed, it is the number-one imported wine in U.S. history with more than 165 million cases sold so far.

The Riunite story began in 1950 when the Italian wine industry was suffering from a postwar crisis and many winegrowers formed cooperatives to make and market their wines, either selling in bulk or under their own labels. It was essentially a defensive strategy because they could not rely upon private wineries to buy their grapes at sustainable prices. Cooperatives were crucial to the survival of wine production across Europe in those days, just as they were during the crises of the 1920s and 1930s. Indeed, they are still important today. It is possible that as much as half of all the wine produced in Europe today and one in four bottles of wine in the entire world comes from the barrels and tanks of cooperative wineries!

It is my understanding that Cantine Cooperative Riunite was formed as a "second level" cooperative, meaning that its nine founding members were local cooperatives themselves, not individual winegrowers. A cooperative of cooperatives. They banded together to share investment costs, spread out risk, and gain economies of scale. The cooperative's bylaws were modified in 1970 to allow individual grower members. According to a 2012 report, Riunite had at that time 3,700 members and twelve wine production centers in Emilia-Romagna plus an additional fourteen thousand members and fifteen associated wineries in other parts of Italy. Riunite is one of the largest "invisible" wine producers in the world.[6]

The key moment in the growth of Riunite was in 1969 when the group signed a ten-year exclusive marketing arrangement with Villa Banfi, a New York wine importer that is now famous for its own high-end Italian wines as well as the global portfolio that it distributes. John F. Mariani, Jr., saw Riunite Lambrusco as a "red Coke" of a wine that might appeal to the great American middle class.[7] The first hundred-case order of Riunite Lambrusco eventually grew to millions of cases. With Banfi's help, Cantine Riunite adapted their product to the American market, raising quality, reducing alcohol levels, and minimizing vintage variation. Banfi worked on packaging and marketing, too, including a very memorable series of television ads with tag lines like "If you haven't tried Riunite you don't know what you're missing" (obvious, but true), and my favorite, "Riunite on ice . . . that's nice."

Lambrusco benefits from chilling and Banfi marketed it as a wine to keep in the refrigerator for ready access. Mariani thought of everything, even introducing a screwcap closure so that a half-consumed bottle could be easily re-closed and put back in the cooler. Much more convenient than a Champagne-style cork and cage. Now, that's nice![8] No doubt about it, Banfi and Cantine Riunite were ahead of their time in terms of adapting to consumer trends and they continued over the years, introducing many variations on the basic Lambrusco including fruit-flavored wine products, which are a hot category these days when even lower alcohol levels (due to the added fruit juice) are much in demand.

Riunite is everywhere here in the United States (Sue spotted it not long ago in a wine display at a gasoline station store near Castle Rock, Washington), but have you tasted it recently? Maybe it's too invisible to show up on your radar. We found standard 750-milliliter and 1.5-liter bottles of Riunite on the bottom shelf of a local supermarket's wine wall ($4.99 and $8.99 respectively) and tried it on ice. It was nice, although I think I like it better as a sangria base. If you haven't tasted Riunite recently you probably don't know what you're missing. For millions of people, it is a wine that put Italy on their personal tasting maps.

OLD FRIENDS AND NEW

Since I am only allowed a relatively few wines on our Italian stop I will turn to some old friends and new. The Antinori wine family is old indeed—Marchesi Antinori counts twenty-six generations of winemaking in Tuscany dating back to 1338, when Giovanni di Piero Antinori was initiated into the Florentine Winemakers' Guild. The family business evolved over the centuries and is led today by Marquis Piero Antinori and his three daughters Albiera, Allegra, and Alessia. The wines range from the very affordable Santa Cristina Toscano IGT red blend that Sue and I will have with dinner tonight to the pathbreaking Super-Tuscan Tignanello. Antinori wines are produced in Tuscany and elsewhere in Central Italy and there are international projects in the United States, Chile, Hungary, Malta, and Romania.

Antinori wines are easy to find in the United States, but my memories are firmly linked to Florence itself and the Palazzo Antinori on Via Tornabuoni. That's where the family opened a restaurant and wine bar called the Cantinetta Antinori in 1957, which became my hangout when I was researching a 1990 book called *Mountains of Debt* (about financial crises in Renaissance Florence, Victorian Britain, and postwar America).[9] You could get any of the Antinori wines by the glass at good prices and the food was great and affordable, too. Perhaps because it was the cheapest item on the menu, I seemed to always order *pappa ai pomodoro* ("bread soup," our favorite waiter always said with mock scorn when I asked for it). When we returned to the Cantinetta a few years later the wines were still there, but the place was filled with upscale Asian tourists rather than the U.S. college students who once had classrooms on the upper floor of the building. And the bread soup was still there. Now the Cantinetta has branches in Zurich, Vienna, and Moscow, spreading the Antinori vision of food and wine internationally. Each is different, but *pappa ai pomodoro* is listed on every one of the menus. I'll pick just one of the many Antinori wines for our list, the

Marchesi Antinori Chianti Classico Riserva DOCG for when great friends come to dinner.

Antinori represents the history of Italian wine and its inextricable link to land, culture, conviviality, and cuisine. It is an old friend in several meanings of those words. My new wine friend is Prosecco. Not because Prosecco itself is new or because we have just discovered it ourselves, but because it has recently taken the world by storm to such a degree that a rumor circulated in London a few months ago that we were drinking the Prosecco tanks bone dry. A Prosecco shortage loomed! The rumor was false but the panic was real. A world without Prosecco? Unthinkable. But only a few years ago it was hardly known at all outside of Italy.

Prosecco is a sparkling white wine from a region in northeast Italy that includes parts of Friuli and the Veneto. It is named for the region and made from the Glera grape using a technique invented in 1878 by Antonio Carpenè, the founder of the famous wine school in Conegliano where I lectured in 2015. A still base wine is made, as with the Champagne method, and a secondary fermentation is created to provide the bubbles, but it happens in a pressurized container (an autoclave) instead of in the bottle. The "Italian method" of sparkling wine provides less direct contact with the yeast and produces wines that are fresh and with good fruit.

We visited a number of producers during our stay in Prosecco-land, including Carpenè Malvolti, Paladin, Ponte (a cooperative), Borgoluce, Bisol (the family behind Venissa), Mionetto, Sorelle Bronca, and Silvano Follador, a tiny operation run by a brother and sister team. Along the way we passed the big La Marca winery, a second-level cooperative that makes the best-selling Prosecco in the U.S. market. Prosecco redefined the way that many consumers think about sparkling wine and has invigorated that market around the world.

What Prosecco wines should we choose for our collection? The choice is somewhat arbitrary since Prosecco comes in many styles, including an interesting student-made still Prosecco that we were given by the professors at the Conegliano wine school. I think I must choose Carpenè Malvolti for its link with history and Silvano Follador for its focus on a particular philosophy of wine, but there are many good choices. What do they all have in common? High quality and great ambition. And Batali's Impossibility Theorem, too. They (and the other wines I have mentioned here) are products of particular times and places. No single wine can hope to represent Italy, but they all express something of its essence.

That's all for Italy. Just time to *fare un Brindisi*, which means to raise our glasses (of Prosecco), to toast Batali's Impossibility Theorem before we resume our round the world expedition.

~

The Wines

Venissa Venezia, Isola di Mazzorbo, Veneto, Italy

Riunite Lambrusco, Emilia-Romagna, Italy

Marchesi Antinori Chianti Classico Riserva DOCG, Tuscany, Italy

Carpenè Malvolti Conegliano Valdobbiadene Prosecco Superiore, Veneto, Italy

Silvano Follador Valdobbiadene Prosecco Superiore di Cartizze Brut Nature, Veneto, Italy

~

Chapter 4

Syria, Lebanon, and Georgia
The Wine Wars

When Phileas Fogg left Italy he headed straight for Cairo and the Suez Canal, which was then and probably still is the fastest route from Europe to India via conventional land and sea routes. The Canal drew Fogg to the Middle East, but a different force beckons us. Wine's history is deeply rooted in this region. Evidence of ancient wine production has been found on Mount Ararat, for example, in what is now Turkey. (Noah's vines on the traditional landing point of Noah's ark? Probably not, but interesting.) And it was the Phoenicians and then the Greeks who carried wine to Italy and France, whence it spread throughout the world. Moving forward on our journey to understand wine's story, it seems that we are also moving backward in wine history.

Phoenicia? Where is that? The Land of Palms, we are told, included territory in modern-day Lebanon, Syria, and Northern Israel. In days long past these places had much in common and wine was high on the list. Don't forget that Jesus famously turned water into wine at the feast of Cana. And that's just the tip of the biblical iceberg as Randall Heskett and Joel Butler reveal in their fascinating book, *Divine Vintage: Following the Wine Trail from Genesis to the Modern Age*.[1] These days the regions have something else in common. Instability. Conflict. War.

WAR AND WINE

Wine and war do not combine very well. Wine needs peace for the tending of the grapes and the harvest, which cannot be delayed or rescheduled to a more convenient place or time. Wines need peace to ferment, mature, and develop. Wine has for centuries relied upon peaceful trade routes to get from point of production to its widespread consumers. If the dove were not such a powerful symbol I would suggest that the wineglass be used to represent peaceful sentiments.

There is little immediate hope for peaceful times and the wines that come with them in Syria and Lebanon and the plan for this chapter was always to investigate the relationship between wine and war here in one of the most unsettled wine regions on earth.

There are many books about wine and war, but they are not always exactly what they seem. My 2011 book is called *Wine Wars,* for example, but it isn't about terrorists so much as *terroirists.*[2] *Wine Wars* examines the war *within* the world of wine. What is wine and what should it be? Is it a mass-produced industrial product conceived by marketing consultants and manufactured to uniform specifications? Or is it a natural product forever tied to particular times and places? Wine is both of these things, of course, and a whole spectrum of things between them, but the battle necessarily rages over which direction wine will evolve—toward the global and the commercial or closer to the "*terroirist's*" natural and local.

The wars I described in *Wine Wars* exist pretty much everywhere that wine is made or consumed and in fact the forces I examined are not really limited to wine. The battle between global and local, to take just part of the argument, exists on many fronts as does the tension between standardization and the individual creator, money and art. But is that war the most important thing in Lebanon and Syria, where mortar blasts and terrorist threats are real concerns? No, there is another book that seems to apply here. It is called *Wine and War: The French, the Nazis, and the Battle for France's Greatest Treasure* by Don and Petie Kladstrup.[3] It is one of the most popular wine books of all time and it is easy to see why.

Wine and War reveals how war affects every aspect of life, even (or perhaps especially) wine. It plots the efforts of French winegrowers to protect their vineyards, preserve their treasuries of fine wine, and to cope with the harsh reality of Nazi occupation during the Second World War. Then, finally, when peace arrives, there is the problem of rebuilding what was lost, a task punctuated by the famous vintage of 1945. Lies, truth, heroes, villains, and traitors—this collection of stories really has it all. Burgundy and Bordeaux figure prominently, of course, as does the Pol Roger Champagne that we used to toast the journey in the first chapter of this book. Hitler ordered that vast quantities of the stellar 1928 vintage of Winston Churchill's favorite wine be shipped to Berlin each month along with millions of bottles of Champagne from other makers and great French wines generally. To the victors go the spoils of war, it is said, but nobody mentioned that sometimes they also get wonderful wine. In any case, this is the kind of war story we have come to this dangerous part of the world to explore.

THE MOST DANGEROUS WINE IN THE WORLD

Domaine de Bargylus may be the most dangerous wine in the world. You will perhaps understand why if I tell you that its vineyards are in Syria, on the slopes of Jebel al-Ansariyé, once known as Mount Bargylus, not far from the Mediterranean coast. Wine was made here for centuries and no less an authority than Pliny the Elder, the Roman "Robert Parker," noted its quality, but the link with war is very strong. Wine boomed in Syria, for example, after the Romans defeated King Mithridates VI in 63 BC and occupied the territory. Wine was already made here, of course, but vineyards were expanded and an active regional wine trade encouraged. The wine industry rose and fell over the centuries according to the policies and beliefs of the ruling state, but somehow wine always found a way to endure, if only on a tiny scale at times.

How did wine survive the long decades of Ottoman rule that began in 1516 and ended four centuries later? The Muslim prohibition on alcohol did not extend to wine for religious purposes, which created an obvious opening for Christian wine producers, and in fact the current Domaine de Bargylus is located quite near to Deir Touma, which translates as the "convent of Thomas." Wine thrived again after the First World War when the Treaty of Versailles put this part of the Middle East under the administration of the French, who split Lebanon off from Greater Syria. Syria gained formal independence in 1946 and the Syrian Arab Republic was established in 1963.

The last fifty years have not been peaceful ones and the situation at this writing is dire. Domaine de Bargylus was insulated to some extent from the violence of the "Arab Spring" civil war, which began in 2011, because the vineyards are located quite near to Latakia, the power center of President Bashar al-Assad. Now armies of the Islamic State have joined the battle and making wine or making anything in Syria is difficult and dangerous. Millions of Syrian refugees have fled the country. And yet, in this very hostile environment, wine is made.

Domaine de Bargylus and its sister winery Château Marsyas in the Bekaa Valley of Lebanon are the result of a family determined to preserve both the wine and the story of wine in Syria. Some of my friends don't believe me at first when I tell them about Domaine de Bargylus and I admit that the story is almost unbelievable. But here it is.

The Johnny R. Saadé family are Orthodox Christians with deep roots in both Syria and Lebanon. The family has been active in commerce since the eighteenth century and, under the direction of Johnny R. Saadé and his sons Karim and Sandro, created a diversified set of businesses including transportation, tourism, real estate, and finance. Since the family lived through the French administration of this territory perhaps it should not surprise that the Saadés got the wine bug. Karim and Sandro began to look for potential wine investment opportunities, perhaps in Bordeaux, their father's early favorite, or the Rhône wines that he loved. In the end they decided to invest close to home in both Syria and Lebanon and hired a "flying winemaker" consultant from Bordeaux, the famous Stéphane Derenoncourt, to advise them on vineyards and winemaking. The focus was on finding the best vineyard sites and then making outstanding wines.

The details of the wines and the wineries is very interesting, but it is the human struggle to grow the grapes and make and sell the wines that I find most compelling. A 2014 report in *Al Jazeera* is typical.[4] Neither the Beirut-based Saadé family nor consultant Derenoncourt could visit the vineyards because of border issues, so they had to rely upon remote control supervision via mobile phone and e-mail. Crates of ripening grapes were rushed via taxi from Syria to Lebanon for analysis until, another report advised, even the taxis could not get through. Rockets hit the winery, taking out both vines and hard-to-replace equipment. Fifteen local employees value their jobs in an area where unemployment rates are high, but the risks are high, too. Cross fire, bombings, and potential kidnappings make this a hazardous work zone.

In August 2014, for example, fighting broke out near the winery between Islamist factions and Assad's forces. Bombs exploded in the vineyards and workers bolted for safety. For a time it wasn't clear if it would be possible to pick the grapes at all, much less at the peak of ripeness. Derenoncourt calls the last three vintages "*vins du guerre*" (wines of war). The conflict threatens the vineyards and the winery directly and the final result of the battle is of great concern. A victory by the Islamic State would introduce their very strict anti-alcohol interpretation of sharia law, which would mean death to the enterprise at the very least and perhaps death to all those involved. To make matters worse, conflict in Syria adds to the instability of the Bekaa Valley, the heart of the Lebanese wine industry and the next stop on our itinerary.

MAN OF THE YEAR

Phileas Fogg's journey around the world in eighty days was carefully scheduled, perfectly organized in theory, but filled with accidents, coincidences, and various random happenstance in practice. Fortune both good and bad played important parts in the unfolding drama and what was true for Jules Verne's character seems to be true for me, too. When I made plans for this chapter I had no thought of Syria or the Saadé family, Domaine de Bargylus or Château Marsyas. Their part of the story was the result of good luck as I worked to learn more about this part of the world. My original plan was very simple. Lebanon was the story of one man and his wine.

When *Decanter* magazine, the UK publication that declares itself to be the "the world's best wine magazine," initiated an annual "Man of the Year" award for "services to wine" in 1984, it had a world of worthy candidates from whom to choose. Indeed "Person of the Year" (as the award came to be called) honorees in future years included Laura and Corinne Mentzelopoulos of Bordeaux in 1985, Marchese Piero Antinori in 1986, Robert Mondavi in 1989, Professor Émile Peynaud in 1990, Michael Broadbent in 1993, May-Eliane de Lencquesaing in 1995, Hugh Johnson in 1996, and Jancis Robinson in 1999. The list of important figures goes on and on.

So it must have come as something of a surprise when the very first winner's name was announced: Serge Hochar of Château Musar of the Bekaa Valley, Lebanon. "No one in the world of wine can have had such an appallingly difficult and dangerous job—and surmounted it," the *Decanter* proclamation reads. "To produce wine at all in the circumstances is remarkable, to produce excellent wine is extraordinary."

Decanter was right to suggest that simply making the wine was a challenge. One of Serge Hochar's great achievements, by his own account, was losing only two vintages to conflict. War prevented the grapes from being harvested at all in 1976 and in 1984 violence disrupted the supply chain and not in a good way. You see the winery is located away from the vineyards, a strategic decision made because of fear of a potential Syrian invasion of the Bekaa Valley. Two trailer-loads of grapes were picked and sent off to the winery, one by road and the other by boat. Both were badly delayed and the grapes started fermenting spontaneously in their bins. The resulting wine was not released in the normal course of business, creating a second war-related void in the vintage lineup. "The wine is a tribute to Hochar's fortitude," write Heskett and Butler, who somehow found a way to taste it, "it is unique and flavorful in a madeirized, earthy-aggressive way."[5] "For others weather is the problem," Hochar said, "For us it is war."

Château Musar was born in 1930 during the period of French administration, the creation of Gaston Hochar, Serge's father. French influence was very strong at this time; during the Second World War Beirut was known as the Paris of the Middle East because of its banking and financial importance and its strong French cultural influence, which extended to wine.[6] Serge himself was born in 1939 and eventually went to work at the winery along with his brother Ronald, who took care of the business side of the enterprise while Serge focused on the cellar. The 1954 vintage was his first in full charge of making the white wines and he took over the reds, too, in 1956. The desire to make the very best wines sent him to Bordeaux, where he studied with another name on the *Decanter* list, Émile Peynaud, arguably one of the most important figures in twentieth-century wine history. Peynaud was a pioneer in what you might think of as a scientific and modernist idea of winemaking who fought vigorously against dirty cellars and seat-of-the-pants winemaking practices. His goal was to produce wines that were consistently clean and vibrant—nothing "funky," nothing flawed—starting with vineyard practices and continuing throughout the production chain.

The problem of making quality wine was replaced with another challenge in 1979, when the instability and violence of a civil war caused the key domestic wine market, which had traditionally absorbed most of the production, to essentially evaporate. Now the issue was how to gain a stronger international reputation for the wines and to reach out even more to export markets. Serge Hochar packed his bags and his wines and hit the road, becoming a most effective ambassador for his wines and the Lebanese industry. "There was scarcely a wine event in the world that he didn't attend," according to Michael Broadbent. "The whole world knew him." A defining moment occurred in 1979 at the Bristol Wine Fair when Broadbent awarded Château Musar 1967 the top prize, gaining it instant recognition in the most important wine market in the world. An article in *Decanter* followed and it is easy to say that the rest is history, but in fact a lot of old-fashioned hard work was required. Château Musar grew to its current fifty-eight-thousand-case production and its global reputation grew as well. The Bekaa Valley is now home to forty wineries, up dramatically from a low of five during the civil war, which is far too few for a region that was once home to a temple dedicated to Bacchus, the Roman god of wine. Serge Hochar certainly did not do this all himself, but his role was significant and worthy, it is universally agreed, of that 1984 *Decanter* honor.

THE NATURAL

I was not able to meet with Serge Hochar before his untimely death in 2014, but I wanted to get a personal sense of the man, and with this in mind, Sue and I met with Bartholomew Broadbent, the U.S. importer of Château Musar's wines. Bartholomew met Serge Hochar through his father Michael Broadbent and developed a close personal relationship, going so far as to call Hochar his second father. I knew what I wanted to ask Bartholomew over lunch and I thought I knew what the reply would be. What is Hochar's lasting legacy—what will he be best remembered for? I was pretty sure that the answer would be the qualities of determination and optimism in the face of war, instability, and mayhem, the qualities for which he received his *Decanter* recognition thirty years before. But I was wrong.

"Natural winemaking," Broadbent said without a moment's hesitation. Serge Hochar will be remembered not so much for the war in Lebanon, he said, as for that other kind of wine war—the *terroirist* type. This caught me by surprise because, although I knew that Château Musar was an early advocate of organic viticulture in Lebanon, I was not familiar with the natural wine movement's acknowledgment of Hochar as a "godfather" of natural wine.[7]

The natural wine movement is to industrial wine what the Slow Food movement is to industrial food, both a protest and an alternative. The idea of natural wine is to minimize manipulation and intervention in both the vineyards and the cellar so that the wine reflects as well as possible the natural conditions that produced it.

Natural wine proponents rely upon both philosophy and chemistry in taking a stand against wine manipulation and intervention through the minimal use of added sulfur dioxide. They walk a tightrope, trying to achieve higher wine quality while risking "funky" or flawed wine. If the wine is not always perfectly clean, it is perhaps something to be appreciated (rather like a delicious organic apple with a few surface blemishes). Natural wine has many fans and many advocates, none more ardent than Alice Feiring, who included Château Musar in her list of iconic natural wines. "Before the late '60s they used no sulfur at all," she writes "after that for a few decades it was just at bottling." Serge Hochar walked the tightrope, risking funk to achieve something special.

The irony of this, of course, is that risking funk and faults is the very last thing that you would expect from a student of Émile Peynaud! Serge Hochar knew the rules, but he didn't subscribe to the conventional wisdom. He was willing to take big risks for big returns, even chancing sometimes getting no vintage at all due to wine and war and taking risks of a different type in the *terroirist* wine wars. This isn't the story that I thought I would tell about wine and war, but it is an inspiring one, don't you think? Serge Hochar "The Natural" and Man of the Year, too.

So what about the wine? Château Musar Rouge is a blend of Cabernet Sauvignon, Carignan, and Cinsault grapes from very old vines. These wines are meant to age (something that critics of natural wine might think impossible) and they are held at the winery to mature much longer than is typical for other wines. I bought a bottle of the 2003 at the Heathrow duty free shop when I passed through in 2014. It was delicious and distinctive, showing its age but in a good way. A tasting note I found for the 2004 vintage included terms such as muddy, funky, gamy, and furry, which the 2003 definitely was not. Descriptors like these are not part of Émile Peynaud's vocabulary, but not foreign to the natural wine lexicon.

GEORGIAN WINE WARS

I was drawn into another combination of wine and war when I was invited to travel to the Republic of Georgia in 2016 to speak at the first United Nations World Tourism Organization (UNWTO) global wine tourism conference.[8] Georgia, the self-styled "cradle of wine," with eight thousand vintages so far and counting, is probably the most wine-centric country on the planet. Just about everyone drinks wine, most families make wine for their own use and to share with friends, and the cultural significance of wine and vine are everywhere to be seen from Soviet-era patriotic monuments to centuries-old church iconography (Saint Nino, who converted the nation to Christianity in the fourth century A.D., fashioned a cross from grapevine cuttings tied with her own hair). If you are organizing a wedding or other celebration in Georgia, we were told, a good rule of thumb is to allow two liters of wine for women and three for men. Really.[9] Georgia is a wine lover's kind of place.

Georgia is no stranger to war. The compact country is located at an important geopolitical crossroads and it is amazing that its language and culture have survived all of the different foreign powers and empires that have invaded but not necessarily really conquered it over the centuries. Georgia has endured and this is true of its wine as well, although the odds were often against it. A long tradition of natural wine production was suppressed during the long years of Soviet dominance. Quantity not quality was the goal and huge factories were built to produce inexpensive semisweet red wines for the Russian market. This pattern did not shift very much in the early years of post-Communist independence since the Russian export market still called the shots. But then a number of Georgians began to experiment with high-quality natural wine production, using organically farmed grapes and made with minimal intervention in the traditional *qvevri*, which are large egg-shaped clay vessels that are buried in the earth for natural temperature control. You see *qvevri* everywhere in Georgia and I think it is both a winemaking tool and a symbol of enduring tradition. Many of the natural wines thus produced are spectacularly good and can be found at restaurants like Noma in Copenhagen, which is often counted among the best fine-dining establishments in the world. Look for Georgian natural *qvevri* wines at natural wine bars near you although I warn you they are produced in tiny quantities and therefore not easy to find. You might need to travel to Georgia to sample them, which is what we did.

Many of the natural *qvevri* wines that we tasted in Georgia were delicate. Their makers eschew sulfites and other preservatives and, like Serge Hochar, they are willing to take some risks to make a statement about wine. The wines are also potentially fragile in an economic sense because of their reliance on external market demand. Georgia is a small country (population about 4.5 million) and a poor one, too. According to the World Bank, Georgia's per capita income is about $3,800 (compared, for example, with $9,000 for Mexico). Rural poverty is a serious problem outside of Tbilisi's bright city lights. The domestic market for high-quality natural wines is therefore limited by their high cost and the ready availability of less expensive home production. Most of the natural wine production is exported to Italy, France, Denmark, Japan, and other wealthy countries. In some ways, therefore, the survival of this element of Georgia's local wine traditions depends on the development of a global market for their products, which seems likely, but in the context of global competition, too. Having survived Soviet dominance, Georgia wine must now negotiate global market capitalism!

I'll add a bottle of natural wine made by the talented, determined, and humble Iago Bitarishivili to our case to honor Georgia's stubborn success. Iago makes just five thousand bottles of this wine each year in his small cellar using the indigenous Chinuri grape. This white wine ferments on the skins so that it is what we usually call an "orange wine," although the Georgians call it "golden" and I think they have it right. It is a good reminder that wine wars are fought on many battlefields and that the good guys sometimes win.

THE WINE THAT WASN'T THERE

I thought I was finished with this chapter when I received an e-mail from Bartholomew Broadbent. Would I like to meet Marc Hochar and taste older vintages of Château Musar? Of course! Marc is Serge's son who manages the winery's commercial side while his brother Gaston makes the wine. Sue and I sat down to taste and talk. What did Émile Peynaud think of your father's un-Peynaud natural wine determination? They had talked about it, Marc said, and Peynaud said he understood and noted the difference between *savoir* and *savoir-faire*. Once you know the rules, you can understand when and where to break them. And that's what Serge Hochar did, even taking matters to the extreme, making wine under all circumstances and from whatever the vineyard gave him, good, bad, or even ugly.

My heart almost stopped when Marc reached into the wine case and pulled out a bottle with the date 1984. That's a wine that doesn't exist, I said. One of the two vintages that wasn't made. No, Marc corrected me, it was made, but not released. Until now.

Curious about the wine, Bartholomew Broadbent asked for a case in 2015 and intended to serve it at a vertical tasting of Château Musar wines. But he opened a bottle and smelled an awful smell—the kind of smell that makes you afraid that you might get really sick if you tasted the wine. He pulled the wine from the program, but returned to it out of curiosity a little later and found it completely changed. "I couldn't believe what I was smelling," he told me. The wine went back into the tasting. "Miraculously, and proof that Château Musar is a living thing, it had become so good over a three-hour period of breathing that it was actually voted the best wine of the lineup." Drinkable at last, the wine was finally released more than thirty years after the grapes were picked.[10]

And so we sipped this wine of war, the one made with grapes that fermented spontaneously on the unplanned slow boat trip to the winery. It looked as old as its years and tasted like a cross between old sherry and port. Interesting more than delicious. A wine to ponder not gulp down. War is the enemy of wine, but this very natural wine has endured, just like the spirit of the man who made it.

⌒

The Wines

Château Musar Red, Bekaa Valley, Lebanon

Domaine de Bargylus Red, Syria

Iago's Wine Chardakhi Chinuri, Republic of Georgia

⌒

Part II
ROUNDING THE CAPE

Chapter 5

Spain

El Clásico

Wine's journey to Western Europe and beyond from its cradle in Central Asia and the Middle East took two distinct paths that bracket the Mediterranean Sea. The northern route went to Greece and then Rome and on to France, throughout Europe and eventually the world. This is how we think of wine, as a beverage with Southern European roots and global reach.

But there was a second road. The Berbers and Phoenicians settled the Mediterranean shores of North Africa, taking their vines and wines with them to the areas that are now Tunisia, Morocco, and Algeria. That's the route we will take on our way to Spain.

NORTH AFRICA'S WINE BOOM (AND BUST)

North Africa? Isn't that the Sahara Desert? Isn't it too dry and hot for wine grapes to grow? Almost. Like Australia's Barossa Valley in the Southern Hemisphere (which lies at an equivalent latitude and proximity to the sea), North African vineyards sit perched on the edge of the desert and shores of the sea. Here vines thrived for centuries, but the industry really blossomed under the influence of the French, who annexed Algeria in 1830. French settlers drank wine, of course, and made it, too. They exported wine to France where it found a ready consumer market. Some of the wines won prizes in French competitions, but most were used as blending wines. Dark, powerful Algerian wines, for example, were blended with thin wines or wines from a weak vintage to make them more appealing. North African wines were the medicine that cured the ailments of French wine.[1]

Investment in North African wines increased when the phylloxera louse invaded French vineyards starting in 1863. Some French winegrowers who saw their futures dying on the vine at home fled to North Africa. Wine production in Algeria rose from about twenty-five thousand hectoliters in 1854 to four hundred thousand hectoliters in 1880, 5 million hectoliters in 1900, and 10 million hectoliters in 1915.[2]

By the time that French vineyards were restored to good health, Algerian wine was so thoroughly integrated into the French wine industry that it seemed impossible to separate them. At the turn of the twentieth century wine accounted for half of Algeria's total exports and a third of the country's national income. French winegrowers lobbied for and received many protective measures ranging from import tariffs to increasingly strict regulations intended to limit blending with North African wine.[3] Despite these efforts, viticulture was by 1960 the largest agricultural employer in Algeria. With about 360,000 hectares (almost 900,000 acres) planted to vine, Algeria was the world's largest wine exporting nation and the fourth largest producing nation after Italy, France, and Spain! Algeria, Morocco, and Tunisia together accounted for two-thirds of all international trade in wine.[4] These North African countries were the OPEC of global wine. Incredible.

What happened to the Great North African Wine Spigot? Algeria's war of independence from France in the 1960s was notoriously brutal and left deep scars on both sides. The wine trade and then wine itself faded away, a trend that accelerated with the rise of Muslim cultural influences. Wine is still made, some of it excellent, but the boom that was is very much over. We can only hope that wine will return to its historical place in this part of the world sometime in the future. I want to add an Algerian wine to our collection because of the unique episode in the history of global wine that it represents, so let me choose a multiregional red blend called Cuvée du Président, which I've heard described as "Château Couscous" because it was at one time ubiquitous in Algerian and "Mediterranean" restaurants in the South of France where piles of fragrant couscous anchored every plate. As remembrance of a time when Algerian wine ran like water in France, it is a worthy addition to our list.

Now on to Spain. Grapes have grown on the Iberian peninsula for thousands of years and the Carthaginians and Romans in turn cultivated them and made wine. Wine persisted even when the Moors invaded in the seventh century. Spanish wine evolved in a distinctly Spanish way in dozens of regions that often had little in common with each other. This leaves us today with a jigsaw puzzle of regions, grapes, and wines including sherry, which is a wine world all its own (and probably deserves a chapter of its own, too). How can we understand Spanish wine (or the wines of Spain, if we invoke Batali's Impossibility Theorem)? I have an idea, but it will make more sense if you are a fan of the Beautiful Game, which we Americans call soccer.

THE RIVALRY

Spain has for years been a puzzle and a paradox to the fans of association football, which is variously called soccer, football, or equivalent local terms around the world.[5] Until recently Spain was a country with great club teams but a disappointing national team (the disappointment ended in 2010 when Spain won the World Cup in Cape Town). How can a country whose local teams excel at the global level fail so badly as a national team? One explanation was that the fierce competition between the local club teams somehow limited the cohesion necessary for a great national squad. Significantly, the rivalries were not just about sport, but about bigger things, which is perhaps why they were and are so defining. The greatest rivalry of them all is called El Clásico: Real Madrid versus Barcelona.

To most global fans tuning in on television, El Clásico is a game between a team with white shirts from Madrid and another with red-and-blue-striped jerseys from Barcelona. But to Spaniards, it is a clash of cultures. Real Madrid represents domination by the central authority in politics, economics, and culture. Before democracy, Real Madrid was the dictator's team, a "soft power" tool for General Francisco Franco to project his authority over Spain's many regions. It is said that Franco didn't much care for soccer, but Real Madrid's success was useful to him and its victories were his, too. In order to win, Real Madrid often relied upon foreign coaches and players (called *galácticos*, or superstars) including Portugal's Cristiano Ronaldo today and the legendary Argentine Alfredo Di Stéfano and Hungarian Ferenc Puskás in past years of glory.

Barcelona has its own team, its own anti-dictator political philosophy, and even its own language. Barcelona the city is the capital of Catalonia, which, along with other regions with strong indigenous cultures, was persecuted by the Franco regime. Sometimes the only way Catalan patriots could protest their oppression was by cheering for their team to win El Clásico. Barcelona also relied upon foreign help, notably Johan Cruyff, who perfected "Total Football" at Ajax and for the Netherlands before playing for and then coaching Barcelona. Today's team includes the South American trio of Argentine Lionel Messi, Uruguayan Luis Suárez, and Brazilian Neymar.

For decades the irony of Spanish soccer was that the teams of El Clásico were great, but the team of Spain was not. Why? The problem was solved but the question not answered by the 2010 World Cup victory, which was won by players from throughout Spain playing a short-passing system that looked to old-timers like a variant of Cruyff's total game. Although Franco is long gone, the tension between the power center of Madrid and the outward-looking, cosmopolitan Barcelona remains. In 2015, for example, Catalonians went to the polls to vote on the question of independence from Spain. Banners of the Catalonian flag (part of the crest sewn onto every Barcelona soccer jersey) flew everywhere and a political breakup was avoided by the tiniest of electoral margins.

ISN'T THIS SUPPOSED TO BE ABOUT WINE?

So what does this have to do with wine? Well, by all rights Spain, with its long history, rich diversity and the largest total area of vineyards in the world, should be recognized as one of the greatest wine nations but until a few years ago it seemed to punch below its weight in terms of global reputation. Why? And what has changed to allow the wines of Spain to rise in world markets?

The soccer metaphor requires that we begin by exploring the wine equivalent of Barcelona and Real Madrid, which works if we are not too literal. Spain's largest wine region is indeed in the center of the country not too far from Madrid and its legendary Los Blancos team. But while La Mancha may be Spain's largest wine region it is not its greatest because it is home to vast plantings of a wine grape named Airén. Are you familiar with Airén? It is Spain's most planted wine grape. Indeed, it is the most planted white wine grape in the world! Even today after thousands of acres of Airén have been grubbed up under European Union wine rationalization programs (and replaced with more marketable wine grapes such as Tempranillo), Airén is number one. The wines that Airén produces can be perfectly good to drink, but they are typically relatively simple and often used for blending with other wines or as a base for brandy production. There is nothing wrong with Airén—every wine region has its everyday workhorse grape—but there is nothing especially memorable about it, either. Not a *galáctico* wine, if you know what I mean.

If we are looking for the vinous equivalent of Los Blancos we need to shift base just a bit to the heart of Spanish red wine. Rioja and Ribera del Duero are home respectively to Spain's most famous red wine type (Rioja) and its most famous wine, period: Vega Sicilia Único.

THE REAL MADRID OF SPANISH WINE

For many wine enthusiasts Rioja and Spanish wine are synonymous, although this is unfair to the country's dozens of other wine-producing regions. Named for the river Oja (Rio + Oja = Rioja), Rioja sits in the northeast, extending a bit into Basque territory. Wine has been made here since the Roman times and was an industry sustained through the years by the monasteries. Production was limited for a long time by the extent of the market, however—Rioja was an isolated region until connected to the center and the coast in the nineteenth century. Production then ramped up quickly for domestic and export markets.

What is interesting to me about Rioja is how much its evolution has in common with Algeria's golden past. French influence and vine disease played leading roles in both cases. When powdery mildew struck French vineyards in the 1840s, for example, wine merchants from Bordeaux came to Rioja to make up for the diminished local supply. Bordeaux varieties including Merlot and Cabernet Sauvignon were planted and added to Tempranillo blends to appeal to the French export markets. When phylloxera struck French vineyards in the 1860s, French influence and export orientation accelerated and French practices such as barrel aging (generally in American oak *barriques*) were introduced and soon defined the region. As railroad transport improved so did exports until, by the end of the nineteenth century, Rioja was known to export as much as 500,000 hectoliters (13.2 million gallons) of wine *per month* to France. Rioja became to Bordeaux what Algeria was to the south of France—a critical source of powerful red wines to fill bottles and store shelves.[6]

Rioja's fortunes declined when phylloxera struck the region starting in 1901 and when competition from export markets generally increased. But the image and reputation of the wines and the region endured even during the period of the Franco dictatorship. The post-Franco era with its greater openness has seen Rioja blossom. Its global markets have expanded while international competition has forced the Rioja producers to push for even higher quality in the vineyard and the cellar.

My choice for a wine from this region is very personal, as wine choices often are. I was speaking at an international wine industry conference in London called Wine Vision in 2014 and had the pleasure to be seated at dinner next to Javier Ruiz de Galarreta, who is president, founder, and CEO of ARAEX Rioja Alavesa & Spanish Fine Wines, an outward-looking company with wineries and vineyards in several Spanish regions. Javier supplied the wines for the dinner and one of them caught my attention as a potential representative of Rioja today. It is called R&G Rolland Galarreta Rioja and those of you who are familiar with flying winemakers will instantly guess that, if the G is for my host Javier Galarreta, the R signifies Michel Rolland, the superstar flying winemaker from Bordeaux. The *galáctico* Bordeaux connection honors Rioja's past while the wine itself says something about its future. A worthy representative of the "Real Rioja" team.

SPAIN'S FIRST GROWTH

To say that a wine is a "first growth" is indirectly honoring a French connection in another way, since the idea of first growths (and seconds and thirds and so on) dates from the Classification of 1855 in Bordeaux. To be a first growth is to be a *galáctico*. To be a nation's sole first growth, as people claim for Vega Sicila Único, is to be beyond category. Pelé, I suppose, or since we are referencing Real Madrid, Ronaldo, Di Stéfano, or Puskás. Super *galácticos* all.

Vega Sicilia is not in Sicily as you might guess. The name derives from *Pagos de la Vega Santa Cecilia y Carrascal* where *pago* refers to a place, a *terroir*, and a *vega* an alluvial plain near a river.[7] The wine comes from the Ribera del Duero region (the same river that is called the Douro in Portugal). The winery is more than 150 years old and this particular wine has been made (only in the best years) for a century, giving it a substantial heritage. Vega Sicilia's status derives from its high quality, of course, but there is also a certain mystique due to its exclusivity. Initially, according to Luis Gutiérrez, the wine was not sold at all. You could only receive it as a gift of the producing family.[8] Personal connection, not money, was the wine's currency. Money does buy the wine today, but sales are strictly controlled. Membership on the winery's allocation list is handed down from parents to children, so openings do not often appear. The bodega also imports one of the world's most sought-after Burgundy wines, the Domaine de la Romanée-Conti and buyers get access to this *galáctico* as well as its Spanish teammate.

MÉS QUE UN WINE?

If Rioja and Vega Sicilia represent the Real Madrid of Spanish, what is the Barcelona? What wine completes a yin-yang pairing that captures the spirit of this complex and dynamic country? It must be white since the other wines are red. It must be democratic, since Vega Sicilia is in every way aristocratic. It must come from Catalonia, of course, and be more than just a wine (*més que un wine*) just as Barcelona Football Club is famously *més que un club* (more than just a club). Like the city of Barcelona itself, it must turn its face toward the world beyond Spain, even as it plants roots in that Iberian country. And, to complete the parallel, it should harbor down deep certain elements that are the same as its opposite. There are several possible candidates for this but the choice for me is clear, Cava, Catalonia's (and Spain's) answer to Champagne.

Cava (like Italy's Prosecco) is a relatively recent innovation, dating to 1872 when José Raventós visited Champagne and returned to Catalonia determined to produce a similar sparkling wine with indigenous Spanish grapes. His family's Codorníu winery dates back to 1551, but its modern history begins with those first bottles made using the traditional method (secondary fermentation in the bottle as in Champagne) rather than the Italian method invented at about this time (secondary fermentation in pressurized autoclaves as with Prosecco).[9] The wines, which we now call Cava, were known as Champaña until 1970, when Spanish authorities finally yielded to French producer pressure to change the name to one that could not possibly be confused with Champagne. Cava wines are made in several regions of Spain, but the wine is most closely associated with Catalonia.

Ironically, just as in Rioja, the development of the Cava industry was stimulated by the death of its vines due to phylloxera in the 1880s. When the vineyards were replanted on phylloxera-resistant rootstocks, the grape varieties chosen where white, not red—Macabeo, Parellada, and Xarel-lo, the Holy Trinity of Cava grapes, although other varieties including those associated with Champagne are now allowed.

To represent Cava I have chosen two very different wines. The Gran Codorníu Gran Reserva honors this wine's original inspiration. It is made from Pinot Noir grapes from a specific vineyard (in Champagne it would be called a Blanc de Noir). It is vintage dated (the current release as this is written is 2007), built to be aged, and makes a statement about Cava's past as well as its future, as producers work tirelessly to increase quality.

The Gran Reserva captures much of the essence of Cava, but it cannot represent this wine on its own because it is perhaps too aristocratic. To capture the democratic dimension I will choose a wine that I have seen thousands of times on store shelves and restaurant lists. It is difficult to miss with its very distinctive black bottle: Freixenet Cordon Negro, a Brut Cava that is often cited as one of the great bargains in the world of wine.

BEYOND EL CLÁSICO

Once El Clásico defined Spanish soccer, and the national team was a bit of a disappointment. Now Spain moves from strength to strength, with fine teams and great players at every level. It is just the same with Spanish wine. World-class wines can be found in Rioja, Ribera del Duero, Catalonia, and in dozens of other regions, too. Spanish wine, like its national soccer team, has become a world champion. This has not happened by accident but rather through the determined efforts of many winemakers to improve vineyards, modernize winemaking, and shift to more market-friendly styles and grape varieties.

This shift—internationalization, some call it—is a tricky business both in Spain and elsewhere in the wine world where it is happening. I have tasted some "international" wines that are nice enough to drink and popular in the market, but seem a bit soulless. They could have been made anywhere and are sometimes difficult to tell apart. The trick that the best Spanish winemakers have mastered, and the foundation for Spain's reputation today, is to make wines that retain their Spanish soul and respect history and *terroir*, drawing upon the best of old and new. These wines give consumers an experience they cannot have anywhere else.

And so I think my soccer metaphor works. The great Spanish national soccer teams of recent years have succeeded because they have mastered this trick, adapting international influences in a distinctively Spanish way, which is also the secret of Spanish wine.

There are so many wonderful and distinctive wines from so many Spanish regions and I am sad that there is not enough to taste and space enough to write about them all. The wines we take with us from this part of our journey tell interesting stories, but what of the wines we must now leave behind? I think I can hear many of you muttering, "Yes! Yes! What about *sherry* in all its wonderful forms? How can the Spanish story end without sherry?"

My answer, which will not satisfy many, is this. Phileas Fogg's journey had many twists and turns and unexpected surprises. Ours is likely to be the same (did you expect to stop in Algeria?). We leave Spain now, but we may not be done with Spanish wine!

⌇

The Wines

Cuveé du Président, Algeria

R&G Rolland Galarreta, Rioja, Spain

Vega Sicilia Único, Ribera del Duero, Spain

Gran Codorníu Gran Reserva, Catalonia, Spain

Freixenet Cordon Negro, Catalonia, Spain

⌇

Chapter 6

Portugal

Any Porto in a Storm

Here is my somewhat embellished story of how the world came to love port wine. Port might not have been discovered in 1678 if France and Great Britain had not been locked in a trade war. High taxes on French imports forced the wine-loving English to look to other sources, including Portugal, which is conveniently situated on Europe's Atlantic coast, a relatively short boat trip from British markets.[1]

With this in mind, it is said, a wine merchant from Liverpool sent his two sons to Lisbon to see if they could find some decent (and tax-advantaged) wines to sell. The sons first traveled up the coast toward Porto (this is where I start to romanticize the story just a bit, but bear with me). There were plenty of wines in this cooler, rainy region, but for the most part they were thin, acidic white wines. If you have ever tasted a Vinho Verde, which comes from this region, you will have some idea of these wines, but Vinho Verde today is made in friendlier style, less acidic than before in part to appeal to market buyers.

Oh no, the brothers said to each other. We can't take these wines back to Father. He could never sell them in Liverpool.

And so, following some advice they were given, they headed up the Douro River until they got to the inland vineyard areas, which were in so many ways the total opposite of the coast. The weather here was hot and the grapes that were grown were high in sugar, low in acid, and had thick skins to protect them from the sun's harsh rays. The wines they produced were dark, tannic, and harsh, the result of the particular grape varieties plus uncontrolled hot, fast fermentation. Oh no, the brothers told each other. These aren't the wines we are looking for either. Father could never sell these wines at home. We have failed!

And so, burdened with bad news, they set off back down the Douro toward Porto and home. They chanced to stop at the monastery at Lamego and, well, they discovered the wine we now call port. The abbott there was making a wine they had never seen or tasted before. The dark red grapes were softly crushed using feet, not presses, releasing deep-colored juice but not harsh tannins. The must fermented as usual but instead of allowing the wine to boil up uncontrollably until all the sugars were gone (the "ferment" in fermentation), a dose of grape brandy was added, which killed off the yeast cells, leaving a sweet, warm, balanced wine. The sweetness was welcome in a world where sugar was still very expensive and sweet wines more respected than they are today. The higher alcohol content was welcome, too, since it would act to safeguard the wines during their inevitable ocean voyage. This was the wine they had been looking for. Success!

The Liverpool brothers didn't invent port, but they did find a previously untapped market for this distinctive wine, which was soon a familiar feature of the British table. In fact, so ubiquitous was port that when the economist David Ricardo sat down to write his famous treatise *On the Principles of Political Economy and Taxation* in 1817, he chose port to illustrate the benefits of free trade. As generations of university economics students have learned over the years, Ricardo's Principle of Comparative Advantage, on which so much trade policy has been constructed, was introduced by showing the benefits of trading British wool for Portuguese wine—port wine, to be sure.

The Douro River is not easy to navigate, so by necessity the business end of the port trade moved downstream from the inland vineyards and winemaking center to the port city of Porto, whence the wine took its English name. Barrels of the wines were brought down the river in small boats, which docked across the river at Vila Nova de Gaia, where "port houses" were built up to age, blend, and eventually bottle the wines before final shipment to market. Many of these houses were organized by British firms, which was natural since Britain was the main export market, and still retain their British names and ownership today. Thus the houses of the very Portuguese port producers

Ferreirinha and Fonseca are joined by such un-Portuguese names as Graham's, Taylor Fladgate, Cockburn, Burmester, Offley, Smith Woodhouse, and Warre. Portuguese wine plus British business and marketing equaled a warm sweet product known around the world.

HERE'S THAT RAINY DAY

I had one free day during my quick visit to Porto to speak to a wine industry group there and as much as I wanted to go up the Douro to the vineyards, which are a UNESCO World Heritage site, a torrential downpour kept me in the city. So I set out to see what sort of wine tourism experience Porto had to offer and I learned a lot. There is much to see and do in Porto itself, but serious wine tourists need to cross the bridge spanning the Douro and enter Vila Nova de Gaia where the port houses are found lined up along the river and up the hillside. My first stop was Quinta do Noval, where I took refuge from the rain and tasted through the wines while drying out. I have to say that there cannot be a better way to warm up than this!

My next destination was Sandeman, one of the oldest and best-known Port houses. You see "The Don," the famous Sandeman logo, everywhere in Porto. Founded in 1790 by George Sandeman, a Scottish wine merchant, Sandeman has interests both in Portugal (port) and Spain (sherry). The Don's distinctive outfit pays tribute to both sides of the business—the Spanish hat paired with the cape worn by university students then and now in Porto (I saw them myself on exam day). If you thought the logo was a tribute to Zorro, think again.

The wine tourism experience at Sandeman begins as you enter the house, which feels and smells exactly like what it is—a grand old warehouse where wines wait patiently in their barrels, often for decades, for the moment when they will be blended, bottled, and go to market. Very atmospheric, immediately communicating a sense of time and place. The first stop once you've come through the great doors is a colorful museum dedicated to Sandeman's success in branding and marketing. The Don might be the most distinctive and instantly recognizable trademark in wine and the museum tells the icon's story from the first images in 1928 through the present day. It's an art exhibit at heart, but with a commercial agenda, and it is interesting to see how the images and messages evolved over the years.

Next came the tour through the big building. The young woman who guided us was dressed as The Don, but she was more professor than student as she made sure, though example and strategic repetition, that we all understood the nature of the different types of port—vintage, LBV, tawny, and so on—how they are made and how they are best consumed. She was very skilled at bringing her students into the story. Walking through the barrel rooms was like walking back in history (which is what we were doing, I suppose), but this is a working operation, not a museum, and we would have seen the cellar hands going about their business if it hadn't been Sunday. The tour ended with an opportunity to taste a couple of wines at long tables adjacent to the cellar-door salesroom and gift shop.

I spent some time talking with a family from Tokyo who were making a European tour and had spent three days in Porto, enjoying experiences like this. Each of the port houses seems to tell its story in a different way, some focusing on their history, others on the production process. Many, like Sandeman and Graham's, offer a variety of tasting experiences in addition to the basic tour. Port pairing seminars (cheese, chocolate) are popular, for example, as well as opportunities to taste tawny port blends of ten, twenty, and forty years or more.

PORTUGUESE WINE INNOVATIONS

Wine is very old in Portugal, going back at least to the Romans. During a visit to the Alentejo region in the south we saw many winemakers working to recreate those Roman wines using very large clay jars that looked like huge handleless amphorae. They reminded me of the *qvevri* we saw in Georgia except they were not buried up to their necks in the earth like the Georgian vessels. It is ironic that a place where wine is so old is also a place where it is changing so fast. Innovation is a driving force in Portuguese wine and it takes many forms.

For wine drinkers of a certain age, Portugal may be best known for an innovative type of wine that has little to do with port. It was introduced in the early years after the Second World War and tailored especially to appeal to wine drinkers in North America. Some say that the target market was initially defined as U.S. military veterans who had served in Europe in the war and developed a taste for the country wines they found there. But soon the market expanded, growing wildly for a time. I am talking about a certain type of fizzy, pink wines that were sold under the labels of Lancers and Mateus Rosé. Sogrape, Portugal's largest winery, makes Mateus while J.M. da Fonseca, an important winery in Setúbal outside of Lisbon, makes Lancers. Mateus, named for a famous Portuguese castle that is featured prominently on the label, started life as a fizzy Vinho Verde but was tailored to its export market, making it sweeter and pink (both white and pink versions were sold). At one time Mateus was the best-selling imported wine in the United States and was amazingly popular in Great Britain, too. By the 1980s Sogrape, which also owns the Sandeman brand today, was exporting over 3 million cases per year. Mateus alone accounted for more than 40 percent of all Portuguese wine exports. Mateus was everywhere, with memorable television spots and celebrity product placement (I stumbled upon a photo of rock star Jimi Hendrix chugging down a half bottle of Mateus).

One of my discoveries while in Portugal was a wine that hasn't changed at all over the years, but that most wine drinkers will see as new and interesting just because they haven't yet discovered it. Bacalhôa Moscatel du Setúbal is made from the Muscat of Alexandria grape, which usually produces sweet wines, but this one is remarkably balanced. The fortified wine sits on its skins gaining tannins for several months and then is aged in oak barrels, sometimes for twenty, thirty, or forty years or more. I've only had the younger wines, but I hope someday to taste one of the older vintages, which are said to be very complex. It is a lovely wine that doesn't cost a fortune. It reminds me that Portugal remains to most wine drinkers an undiscovered land. The Portuguese have been making this wine for more than seven hundred years. I don't understand how those Liverpool brothers missed it.

NO WINE BEFORE ITS TIME

Port, which is Portugal's signature wine, is an example of a wine category that is both timeless and highly innovative. Timeless in the sense that port wines have in many ways remained much the same since their happy "discovery." White ports, ruby ports, tawny ports—in fundamental respects these are the same today as they were a hundred or two hundred years ago. Almost nothing is as traditional as port, with its stenciled bottles and historic brands. And most port wines are timeless in another sense because, like most Champagne wines, they are blends of several regions and several years, with each brand aiming for a consistent "house style" for each wine rather than letting each vintage's individuality show through. This is a plus and also a minus. The plus of course is in terms of branding—only Champagne was a stronger brand than port from a name-recognition standpoint. But it's a minus, too, because that brand, along with sherry, is wrongly associated with one-note sweet wines. Like Rodney Dangerfield, they sometimes don't get the respect they deserve.

And it is a minus because the very best port wine styles are exercises in patience in a very impatient world. Tawny ports must be held by the maker until they are mature in ten, twenty, thirty, or even forty years. That's a lot of time to wait with the investment time-clock running. Vintage ports need time, too, but this time the buyer is expected to patiently wait for the wine to mature. After a certain time of life, buying a newly released vintage port is like planting a tree—an act of faith and hope that you will still be around to enjoy it when it matures. Time is port's friend because of what they do together in terms of the quality of the final product but, from an economic and market standpoint, time is also an inconvenient enemy and seemed to limit port's potential in the postwar years.

One answer to the time problem was an innovation that appeared in 1970, when Taylor Fladgate released their 1965 Late Bottled Vintage (LBV) Port. LBV has the character of vintage port but is ready to drink when released four to six years after the vintage, not twenty years later. It was not quite the Château Cash Flow killer app of the wine world, but it certainly breathed new life into the port market at a moment when this was especially welcome. Some say that LBV saved the port industry when Taylor's Alistair Robertson conceived it.

So far I have focused on product innovation but I haven't mentioned process innovation and that is a mistake, as I learned from a winemaker during my stay in Porto. George Sandeman of the famous port and sherry family invited me to taste through the Ferreira line of wines and ports and of course the Sandeman ports. How could I resist? Even better, we would be joined by Luís Sottomayor, Porto Ferreira's award-winning winemaker. The bottles and glassware filled the big table as we began to taste through the Casa Ferreirinha wines, then the Ferreira and Sandeman ports. The wines were eye-opening. From the most basic wines selling for just a few euros on up to the super-premium products, they were well-balanced, distinctive, and delicious.

"Delicious," I wrote next to the note for the Casa Ferreirinha Quinta da Leda red, which comes from an estate vineyard just one kilometer from the Spanish border. It is the product of a small winery located within the company's larger facility. Spectacular wine, special *terroir*, I wrote.

As we tasted through the ports I started to talk about innovation: new wine styles, rediscovered wines, and so on. Sotomayor stopped me in my tracks. If you want to really understand innovation in Portugal, he said, you have to look beyond new products to the work that is being done to improve the process in the vineyard and the cellar. This is where the real gains are, as seen in the table wines I had just tasted and the ports I was about to sample.

Taste this LBV, Sotomayor said. The LBVs we make today are of the same quality as the vintage ports we made fifteen years ago. And the vintage ports are that much better, too. New products are part of the story of Portuguese wine innovation, but improved winegrowing and winemaking are just as important now and probably more important in the long run. Lesson learned! I came away from the tasting both richer and poorer. Richer because Sotomayor's lesson about innovation will save me some money—as much as I enjoy vintage port, I now have LBV centered on my radar screen and it sells for a good deal less.

And poorer? Well, Sandeman and Sotomayor set up a little experiment for me, first letting me taste their ten-year-old tawny ports and then the twenty-year-olds. We like the twenties, George Sandeman said, because you can taste where they've been (the ten-year-old wines) and also where they are going (the forty-year-old tawny that I tasted next). The tension between youth and maturity makes the twenty-year-old tawny particularly interesting, he said. And I am sad to say that I could taste exactly what he was describing. Sad? Yes, because twenty-year-old tawny costs a good deal more than the ten, and for the rest of my life I am going to be paying that extra sum!

One last innovation to mention before we leave Porto. Wine cocktails are a popular innovation these days, with the Aperol spritz leading the way. Light, fun, and refreshing, wine cocktails are hard to resist on a hot summer day. So we were pleased to discover a new drink in Porto, a white port spritzer, made with equal parts white port and tonic water, served over ice with a slice of lemon or lime. A perfect sundowner drink at the end of a hard day (or an easy one, too). And an innovative way to introduce consumers to traditional port's delicious white sibling.

LIVING HISTORY IN MADEIRA

Portugal is not just a destination on our journey around the world; it is also a jumping-off point, because the Portuguese are noteworthy for their global reach. Is Portugal the world's most global nation? Difficult to prove, but Martin Page makes a strong case in his book *The First Global Village: How Portugal Changed the World.*[2] I read Page's book on the flight to Lisbon and it made me remember Portuguese influences in so many places. Portuguese church services in New England? Portuguese seafood restaurants in Cape Town and Honolulu? The Portuguese trading port of Macau? And of course Goa, Portugal's outpost in India. Have you visited a Japanese restaurant and said *arigato* to thank the waiter when he served your tasty tempura meal? You can thank the Portuguese for both the meal and the term. *Obrigado* is Portuguese for thank you and it was transferred with the tasty food to Japan along with so much else by Portuguese Jesuit priests. Portugal is everywhere and we can follow their pathways on our journey of eighty wines.

The Madeira Islands are pretty remote. According to the *Oxford Companion to Wine* (my go-to reference for facts like this), these Portuguese isles are about a thousand kilometers from mainland Portugal and 750 miles from the coast of North Africa. Ironically, a location far out in the Atlantic Ocean was a key to Madeira's success during the colonial era because it was a perfect provisioning stop for traders going to or from Europe, Africa, the Americas, and of course those on the way around the Cape of Good Hope to India and beyond.

Wine is one of the commodities that the trading ships sought out and so vines were planted where possible on Madeira and winery operations established. The wines thus created, like most wines of the time, did not last very long in the hot hold of a sailing ship so, as with port, alcohol was added to stabilize the wines and thus an industry was created.

Not only did the fortified madeira wines survive long voyages in hot ship holds, they seemed to actually benefit from the treatment. The wines changed ("maderized" is a specialized wine term) and developed in very distinctive ways during the hot, rough voyages. Shipped wines were more valuable than fresh wines and wines that had made the long voyage to the East or the West and then back again (acting as ballast more than cargo) were the most sought after of all.

The market for madeira wines quickly expanded from the crews of the ships that stopped at Funchal, the main city, to consumers in the ports of call. The eighteenth-century version of a global madeira boom took place, with America firmly at its center. As David Hancock explains in his excellent 2009 book, *Oceans of Wine: Madeira and the Emergence of American Trade and Taste,* madeira was virtually ubiquitous in the American colonies.[3] The signing of the Declaration of Independence was toasted with madeira wine!

The rising market for madeira necessitated both vineyard expansion and production innovation. It was not really practical to have dozens of ships sailing around with pipes (as the containers are called) of madeira on board simply to condition the wine. So special facilities were constructed to mimic the ocean effect to a certain extent, especially through prolonged heating of the wines. Heated rooms kept the madeira pipes at about 100°F. The best wines, it is said, are stored high up among the rafters of the lodges where the temperature is naturally high and the sea breezes are felt.

The madeira industry has seen its share of ups and downs since the days when John Adams and Benjamin Franklin drained their cups of the stuff. Vine disease, especially phylloxera, limited supply and then Russian Revolution and American Prohibition destroyed demand at various times. Madeira's market is smaller now than in its heyday but interest is rising.

I have two favorite madeira moments (I remember the people and places even more than the wines). We visited with Bartholomew Broadbent at his offices in Richmond, Virginia, and he gave us a bottle of a youthful Broadbent Madeira, which we shared with Sue's parents and their neighbors that night. They loved the wine and we loved sharing it with them.

Because it is fortified and conditioned in its unique way, madeira wines can last for decades, so the second memorable wine was an 1875 Barbieto Malvasia Madeira served at the end of dinner with my grad school mentor at the Herbfarm Restaurant in Woodinville, Washington.[4] This was for some time the oldest wine on my personal list. That wine has to go on the eighty wine list.

PICK A DIRECTION?

Which way next on our journey? We could go west by northwest to the United States, drawn by the madeira trade's strong colonial currents. Or take a more southerly route to Portuguese-speaking Brazil, where madeira was once all the rage and where a vibrant wine industry now exists.

Brazil is tempting, that's for sure, but I hear Phileas Fogg calling my name. He's headed for India and we need to join him there. So let's head south, stopping perhaps to do some business in Angola, which is a good market for Portuguese wine, or elsewhere in Africa, but with our compass pointed toward Cape Town and then on to India.

⁓

The Wines
Mateus Rosé, Portugal

Taylor Fladgate LBV Port 1965, Douro, Portugal

Sandeman Vintage Port 2011, Douro, Portugal

Bacalhôa Moscatel du Setúbal, Setúbal, Portugal

Barbeito Malvasia Madeira 1875, Portugal

⁓

Chapter 7

Out of Africa

It is only about three hundred miles as the seagull flies from Funchal, the Madeira capital, to Lanzarote in the Canary Islands, our next stop, but a different wine world awaits. Madeira is Portuguese, for example, while the Canary Islands belong to Spain. Rain—too much of it—is Madeira's problem because the warm damp climate encourages all sorts of fungal vine diseases. Hardly any rain at all falls on Lanzarote. And while it is the production technique that makes Madeira so interesting, it is the vineyards that capture your imagination on Lanzarote.[1] Imagine what vineyards would look like on the moon—that's Lanzarote!

Lanzarote is a popular tourist destination—cruise ships stop here all the time, but you would never think to grow wine grapes here if the vines did not already exist. Lanzarote lies about sixty miles off the coast of Africa.[2] The soil—well, there almost isn't any because the island was created by repeated volcanic eruptions and the black rubble or grit doesn't seem like it would support much life. Rainfall is meager at best and the hot winds that blow off the Sahara Desert somehow manage to reach here. Grapevines in the wild like to grow where trees rise up so they can use them as trellises to reach up toward the sun. There are precious few trees on Lanzarote for wild grapes to climb.

And yet grapevines grow on Lanzarote and wine is made. Large conical depressions are dug into the black *picon* volcanic ash with one to three vines planted at the bottom, where they are sheltered a bit from the harsh winds and can benefit from whatever rainwater runs into the crater. Low crescent stone walls offer further protection on the windward side. Some of the vineyards are planted in more conventional patterns where the vines are familiar even if the setting is not, but these "craters of the moon" vines are fantastic.

But the hard work and determination of the Lanzarote *vignerons* would go unrewarded were it not for *picon's* particular property. *Picon* pulls moisture out of the hot, dry wind in the same way a heat pump pulls warmth out of even the coldest winter's day's air. *Picon* has the hydrostatic ability to condense what moisture there is in the dry air and fix it to the layers below, where the vines' roots search it out. As I wrote in *Extreme Wine,* if there are vineyards on Prospero's island where Shakespeare's play *The Tempest* is set, I think they must look and work like this.

I never thought I would taste wine from Lanzarote, but then two friends announced that they had booked a cruise through the Canary Islands and would be stopping there.[3] They brought back a sophisticated, dry, barrel-fermented white wine—made from the Malvasía Volcánica grape by El Grifo, the oldest winery in the islands, founded in 1775. "Resting on its own lees," the label proclaims, "it acquires the flavor and aroma of the volcano." It was distinctive, well balanced, and simply delicious. If any wine truly reflects its *terroir* it is this one!

KENYAN PINOT NOIR?

The obvious next step is to sail on to Cape Town, but I cannot resist a detour to Kenya. Looking at the map of Africa, the obvious places to grow grapes and make wine are at the extremes—Mediterranean North Africa and South Africa's Cape Winelands, but what about Africa's core—the vast area between the more temperate extremes? Too hot and unsuitable for grapevines? Yes, undoubtedly. But that doesn't mean that grapes don't grow and wine isn't made by those determined to do so.

Africa Uncorked: Travels in Extreme Wine Territory by John and Erica Platter is one of my favorite wine books, perhaps because, like the book you are holding now, it takes the form of a journey.[4] The Platters are famous for their annual *Platter's South African Wine Guide,* but their interest in African wine extends well beyond those borders and their 2002 book summarizes a journey in search of the good, bad, and ugly of African wine. Their itinerary took them to the north, where we have already been, finding wine in Morocco, Algeria, Tunisia, and Egypt, to the south, Zimbabwe, Namibia, and South Africa, up to the islands of the continent's eastern shore, Madagascar, Réunion Island, and Mauritius, and finally to East Africa, Ethiopia, Tanzania, and Kenya.

While in Kenya, the Platters paid a visit to an old acquaintance of John's— they had gone to the Duke of York School in Nairobi at the same time in the 1950s. It was Richard Leakey, the celebrated paleoanthropologist and conservationist member of the famous Leakey family who have made so many discoveries about the African origins of the human species. It was more than a social call, however. Leakey along with his daughter Louise farms Pinot Noir on steep hillside vineyards and makes wine from the grapes.

"Well, I am one of those stubborn buggers who don't like to be told it's impossible," Leakey told the Platters in explanation of the vines and wines. Pinot Noir is notoriously difficult to grow anywhere and perhaps especially near the equator in East Africa. But there it was. The vineyard is called Ol Choro Onyore, the Masai name for the ridge where the vines are planted, and the winery itself eventually took the name Il Masin. Louise Leakey recorded the winery's activities on a blog called Zabibu.[5] How are the wines? The Platters' notes say that the 2001 Pinot was their favorite African tropic red, juicy, authentic, and full on the palate. "Nit pickers might focus on the slight attenuated finish and the rather quiet nose," they write, "but it is a triumph under the circumstances." Indeed.

I have to rely upon the Platters' tasting note because I have not and probably never will taste an Il Masin wine myself. In fact, I admit that I am not completely certain about the operational status of the winery today. Louise Leakey's blog ends in 2011 and her winery Twitter account stops a few months later. I suspect that the focus on the winery has yielded to an ambitious new project called the Turkana Basin Institute, which combines serious anthropological research with education (it is affiliated with Stony Brook University in the U.S.) and even a bit of luxury "fossil hunter" tourism designed to raise money and awareness to support the project.[6] But a 2015 *Financial Times* "Lunch with the FT" interview with Richard Leakey reveals that the winery is still alive, producing Pinot Noir and Chardonnay. They try to hide a few bottles from themselves, Leakey says, so that they don't drink it all up before it has time to develop a bit.[7]

There is much more to Kenyan wine and tropical African wine than Château Leakey, which is why John and Erica Platter wrote a whole book about it, but at the moment the heart of Africa is more important as a market for wine than as producer. Sub-Saharan Africa, with its rapid if uneven economic growth and expanding middle class, is widely seen as a wine market of the future. Portuguese wine producers, for example, look to Angola, a former Portuguese colony, for rising sales. Angola is Portugal's number-one export destination, although falling oil export revenues have taken some of the shine off this market in recent years.

Who will rule the African wine market of the future? Many aspire to the throne, but my money is on South Africa. Here's why.

GOING TO EXTREMES IN SOUTH AFRICA

"Today, God be praised, wine was pressed for the first time from Cape grapes."[8] The date was February 2, 1659. The author was Jan van Riebeeck, commander of the Cape Town settlement established by the Dutch East India Company. The wine was mainly Muscadel—fragrant and tasty, according to van Riebeeck, although there wasn't much of it in that first batch, but that would change as production ramped up to satisfy the thirst of not just the local population but also to reprovision ships that called at Cape Town on their way between Europe and Asia. South African wine is surprisingly old and some of the grape-growing farms, as vineyards are called here, have been in family hands for centuries.

One of the earliest wines was made at Governor Simon van der Stell's farm at Constantia, which lies just over Table Mountain from Cape Town itself.[9] The original property has been divided in recent years and two wineries share the famous name: Groot Constantia and Klein Constantia. We visited both on our last trip to South Africa and found that they each preserved something of South Africa's rich history in their own way. Groot Constantia functions as both a winery and a museum and gives a strong sense of place with its restored Dutch colonial buildings and the view over the vineyards down toward False Bay. It is owned and operated by a trust created to preserve this important part of South African history.

Klein Constantia's architecture is impressive, too, but its historical contribution is made through its wines, especially the famous Vin de Constance.

This sweet wine, made from the ripest Muscat de Frontignan grapes, was one of the most celebrated beverages in the world during the eighteenth and nineteenth centuries—the king of wines and the wine of kings. Napoléon Bonaparte famously favored it during his exile on St. Helena. Phylloxera put an end to this wine as it devastated South Africa's vineyards at the end of the nineteenth century. Great effort by Klein Constantia's determined owners and talented winemakers has revived this bit of living history. How does it taste? The reborn Vin de Constance has won many prizes and much praise. It certainly is delicious, but it is almost impossible to know how its taste compares with the storied wines of the past.

Almost? Well, as readers of my previous wine books will know, I have been fortunate to taste one really old South African wine that probably gives a sense of what those old wines were like. It was made around 1800, when Thomas Jefferson was still alive, and it is not impossible that Jefferson himself might have sipped this wine or one much like it when he was U.S. minister to Paris. The wine is Joubert Muscat d'Alexandrie and the winemaking Joubert family, whose roots go back deep into South African history, have just one barrel of the wine stored in the cellar of their house near Barrydale. Every year they draw off a little of the wine and add a little fresh wine in a sort of solera style. A few lucky people are invited to taste the wine or to purchase a tiny bottle of it at charity auctions. Sue and I number ourselves among the luckiest, tasting this bit of history both with the Joubert family at dinner and then, guided by Cobus Joubert, directly from the barrel down in the dark musty cellar where it lives.[10]

Although wine in South Africa is very old, it might be said that the current wine industry itself is relatively young, dating from the political reforms that ended apartheid and opened South Africa to the world and the subsequent dismantling of the KWV state wine monopoly, which had stifled innovation and investment. The brave new world of South African wine, led by pioneers like Norma Ratcliffe, Danie de Wet and Dr. Paul Cluver and powered on today by a group of ambitious "young guns," seems to move from strength to strength.

There are so many great wines made in South Africa today that it is difficult to choose one or two (or ten!) to represent the new era, but I know one that will do. It is the 2008 Black Label Pinotage from Kanonkop (the name refers to the defensive cannon that was once stationed on the vineyard hill or "kop"). Pinotage is South Africa's distinctive red grape, a cross of Pinot Noir and Cinsault (traditionally called Hermitage hereabouts) created at the University of Stellenbosch nearly a hundred years ago.

This particular wine comes with a story. We were in Stellenbosch for some talks I was giving and Johann Krige happened to pour a glass of the Kanonkop Pinotage for Sue. She sniffed and sipped and smiled. "This is South Africa's Hill of Grace," she proclaimed. If you do not know about Hill of Grace, well, just wait. I will tell you about it when we get to Australia. Krige *did* know Hill of Grace and it was for him the ultimate compliment! We found a gift bottle at our table the next morning. Like Henschke Hill of Grace, the Black Label comes from a very specific vineyard block, this one planted in 1953. And like Hill of Grace it commands both respect (it is considered to be a South African "first growth") and a premium price.

TWO FACES OF SOUTH AFRICA AND ITS WINE

South Africa is a nation of great contrasts that go well beyond the old and new. It is impossible not to be moved by the challenge of deep poverty that coexists with fantastic economic success. We saw both extremes on a side trip we took from prosperous Stellenbosch down to the Cape of Good Hope. Halfway between the comfortable university town and the fancy villas on the beachfront we drove by South Africa's largest and fastest-growing township, Khayelitsha. The settlement is vast, extending into the distance as far as the eye could see, with a population of four hundred thousand and one of the lowest average family incomes in the region. The poverty and associated health and social problems are daunting.[11]

The two faces of South Africa are reflected in its wine industry.[12] Our final day in the Cape Winelands, for example, was spent in the luxury of the Rupert family's wine holdings. Anton Rupert, who died in 2006, was an incredible entrepreneur who, starting with just pennies in his pocket, accumulated a fortune counted in the billions of dollars from businesses in various fields including tobacco and luxury goods. The Rupert's Swiss-based Richemont holding company controls a portfolio of luxury product brands including Cartier, Alfred Dunhill, and Montblanc. The family also has important investments in the beer, wine, and spirits sector in South Africa, including a major stake in Distell, the largest wine producer.

Although Anton Rupert apparently preferred simple, inexpensive wines himself, he and his children are responsible for some of the Cape's most luxurious wine estates and we enjoyed the hospitality at historic La Motte with its great restaurant and at the Cape classic Antonij Rupert wine estate in Franschhoek. It was a special treat to taste the wines at Rupert & Rothschild (a partnership between two famous families) with cellarmaster and CEO Schalk-Willem Joubert (the brother of Cobus Joubert, who took us into the cellar to taste his family's ancient wine).[13] We particularly enjoyed the Rupert & Rothschild Baroness Nadine Chardonnay, which I have added to our traveling collection.

The Rupert family's wines are expensive by South African standards and so are seen as luxury products, not mass-market commodities. La Motte and Rupert & Rothschild find a good market in China, for example, where luxury and status are especially appreciated. I choose them to represent one face of South African wine (and wine in general), although there are many posh wine estates with beautiful grounds and excellent restaurants that could fill the bill just as well.

The Van Loveren Family Vineyards in Robertson, for example, ticks all the luxury wine boxes, especially when it comes to the beauty of its gardens. We stopped there because I wanted to meet Phillip Retief, one of four cousins who manage the vineyards and cellars and run the business, because we were speaking at the same wine industry meeting and I wanted to learn all I could from him. Van Loveren is South Africa's largest family-owned winery and has navigated the twists and turns of the country's evolving marketplace very effectively.

We tasted through the excellent Christina Van Loveren wines and talked about the changing Cape wine scene. And then I asked if we could try a wine that was not on the table but I had heard about constantly since our plane set down in Cape Town. Could we try the Four Cousins? Yes of course came the smiling reply.

Four Cousins wine, which is one of the best-selling brands in South Africa, came about in 2000 when the four Retief cousins got the crazy idea to make an entry-level wine that would appeal to students, newcomers, and anyone with a tight budget.[14] Four Cousins brand was launched in 2005. The 1.5-liter glass bottles were adorned with the Four Cousins name (in English, not Afrikaans as you might expect) and photo portraits of the four cousins themselves.

The wine itself was sweetish, to appeal to consumers not accustomed to the tannins and acidity that can turn some newcomers away, but of a high commercial quality—clean, correct, and balanced.[15] It would remind an American of a Beringer White Zinfandel, Two-Buck Chuck, or perhaps Barefoot, all extremely successful wine brands.[16]

It is probably not a surprise that Four Cousins wine was a success in its target audience of young and new mainly white aspirational consumers. What *was* a surprise was its popularity in the mainly black townships like Khayelitsha, where wine was far from the alcoholic beverage of choice. Four Cousins changed that. Walk into a township tavern and hold up four fingers, we heard, and a glass of Four Cousins will appear. Four Cousins has helped create a new face for South African wine among black South Africans.

I have showed the Four Cousins labels to many people here in the United States and they always shake their heads. Terrible, they say. It will never work. You can't sell a wine anywhere with the photos of four white guys on the label. How could it work in South Africa, a country where racial issues are never far below the surface? Well, there really are four cousins who are responsible for the wine, which gives a measure of authenticity to the story, and if they are willing to put their faces on the product how could it be bad? More than ten million bottles are sold each year. Exports account for a fifth of production.

Exports? Well, yes. Phillip Retief reports growing sales in the Netherlands, China, Brazil, the United States, and New Zealand. But I think he is proudest of Four Cousins' success in the fourteen other African markets where the wine is sold, including especially Uganda, Kenya, Zambia, Namibia, Nigeria, and Ghana. Africa is no longer the economic basket case that many imagine, with the second fastest regional growth rate after China in recent years and a rising middle class in many areas. These facts have got the attention of wine producers around the world who have now integrated Africa to their strategic plan. I think that's why we saw a bottle of Gallo's Barefoot wine on a Stellenbosch supermarket shelf next to Four Cousins.

Is Africa wine's next frontier? The huge consumer market potential is too tempting for global wine producers to ignore. But in terms of wine production, the answer is no, not the *next* frontier. Wine has been here for hundreds of years! Time for the world to rediscover African wine.

So what is African wine? Is it the history of Klein Constantia, the geography of Lanzarote, the determination of Richard Leakey, the "grand cru" excellence of Kanonkop, the aristocracy of the Ruperts, or the democracy of Four Cousins? Easy answer. All of these and more.

Wine in Africa is at once very old and excitingly new. Wine's next frontier? Yes, but not the only one because the places and faces we associate with wine are changing very quickly. Consider that a prelude to the next chapter, which will take us deeper into the future of wine.

〜

The Wines

Klein Constantia Vin de Constance 2011, Constantia, South Africa

Kanonkop Black Label Pinotage 2008, Stellenbosch, South Africa

Rupert & Rothschild Baroness Nadine Chardonnay 2015, Western Cape, South Africa

Four Cousins Sweet Rosé, South Africa

〜

Chapter 8

India and Beyond

New Latitudes, New Attitudes

The conventional wisdom holds that *Vitis vinifera* wine grapevines grow best in the moderate climates roughly defined by two global climate bands—I call them the wine belts—that circle the globe between about thirty and fifty degrees of latitude north and south. The northern belt includes the famous Old World European producers, New World California, and what you might call the New New World of wine in China. The same conventional wisdom suggests that wine in the southern hemisphere is pretty much limited to Chile, Argentina, the tip of South Africa, parts of Australia, and most of New Zealand.

It is possible to make wine outside the wine belts, according to this view, but special circumstances are necessary. Elevation can compensate for latitude in some circumstances, for example, which is why mountain-high Salta in the Argentine north makes some brilliant wines. High elevation affects temperature, increases diurnal variation, and intensifies sunlight—all good things for quality wine at an otherwise marginal latitude. South Africa's winelands are right at the edge, too, but benefit from cool winds coming off Antarctic currents, which make possible cool-climate Rieslings and Pinot Noir in Elgin and other favored areas.

The economist John Kenneth Galbraith used to say that the conventional wisdom is always wrong and this is proving to be true for the latitude theory of wine. *Vitis vinifera* vines are being grown, and better and better wines are being made in areas once thought horribly wrong for good wine. Some of this progress is due to climate change, which is shifting the borders of the world wine map generally (more about this in a later chapter), but much credit goes to a movement to develop specialized viticultural techniques to grow quality grapes in the tropics.

The movement's name, New Latitudes Wine, was coined by the Thailand-based wine writer Frank Norel at a 2003 conference in Bangkok. Writing in 2004, wine critic Jancis Robinson expressed her amazement about the number of vineyards and wineries that were sprouting up close to the equator. "I still find it hard to believe that New Latitude Wines will ever be seriously good," she wrote, "but then that's what was said about New World Wines not that long ago."[1] Attitudes toward the wine and the winemaking can change, even if the latitudes themselves are fixed parameters.

SOME ENCHANTED WINE

Bali? Why is our next stop Bali? Well, I suppose a case could be made based upon historical trade routes. Many of the ships that called at Cape Town centuries ago sailed on spice trade routes that took them to this part of the world. Cape Town to Bali or thereabouts is not a ridiculous idea.

But we are here for the wine.[2] Bali wine? Do you mean like Bali Ha'i, the brand of tropical fruit–flavored California wine that Italian Swiss Colony introduced to the U.S. market back in the 1960s? If memory serves (and it was a long time ago) it was a cross between sangria and Hawaiian Punch. No, I don't think that wine had anything whatsoever to do with Bali itself. The inspiration was the famous song from the Rogers and Hammerstein musical *South Pacific*. There is wine in Bali and, against all odds, some of it is good enough to enjoy on your next enchanted evening. The fact of Bali's location, just eight degrees of latitude from the equator, makes wine of any kind an unexpected find for the tourists who consume much of it. And the fact that Bali is in Indonesia, the world's most populous Muslim country, adds to the mysterious enchantment.

There were six wineries in Bali in 2014 according to the *Oxford Companion to Wine*. Hatten Wines, founded in 1994, is the oldest and largest, producing a million bottles a year. Its Hatten label wines are made mainly from Belgia and Alphonse-Lavallée grapes grown on the north island using tropical viticultural practices including pergola-trained vines to cope with humidity and produce three crops a year. Its Two Islands brand wines are made from frozen grapes imported from South Australia. Belgia and Alphonse-Lavallée are not exactly household names for wine drinkers more familiar with Cabernet and Chardonnay, but they were chosen because of their ability to resist tropical vine diseases and thrive in the warm, moist climate.

Sababay Winery opened its doors (overlooking Saba Bay) in 2012, its website going live at 7 am on July 7th of that year (just for good luck). Sababay's owners hope to open a new chapter in the history of Bali wine, with wine made from *Vitis vinifera* grapes grown to an international standard using sustainable practices. Quite a challenge. I was therefore delighted when I had an opportunity to taste their White Velvet wine made from locally grown Muscat grapes. It was light and fragrant on its own but really came alive when we tasted it with a curried seafood dish of the type you might be served in Indonesia. A nice surprise!

I was fortunate when one of my former students, Ali Hoover, travelled to Bali in 2014 and agreed to visit Sababay Winery and report back her findings. Grapes are plentiful in Bali, she discovered, but not the good *Vitis vinifera* grapes you need for fine wines. She found instead that "low-quality grapes considered unfit for consumption flood the Balinese market, destined for the omnipresent sidewalk religious offering." These are not the grapes you are looking for if you want to make quality wine and these are not the grapes used at Sababay.

Getting good grapes took a determined effort. Climate might be a barrier to quality grape production in Bali, Ali wrote, but poor viticultural practices were also to blame, which limited both grape production and rural income growth. In fact, a the local grape industry fell into crisis in the early 2000s due to a combination of vine disease, poor harvests, and marketing woes. Farmers borrowed at high interest rates and fell increasingly into debt. Evy Gozali and her mother Mulyati established the Asteroid Vineyards Partnership in 2010 to address this growing economic and even social crisis. In exchange for agricultural and technical support, 175 Northern Balinese grape farmers committed their crops exclusively to Sababay. Improved farming practices resulted in both higher yields and rising rural incomes for the partnership members.

Who would have thought that wine would be the solution to the problems of struggling small farmers on a tropical Indonesian island? But wine grapes are obviously more valuable than low-quality grapes fit only for ritual use, and the Gozali family's investment in modern and sustainable viticultural training, winery technology, and know-how obviously adds value all along the product chain. Wine is many things—an art, a craft, a healthy beverage, an intoxicating drink—and it can also be tool of economic and social change. Who knew that wine could do so much?[3]

One of the things that Ali liked best about Sababay was that the wines seemed authentically themselves, with a strong Indonesian identity. "Sababay produces wine to match the cultural preferences and local flavors," she wrote. "The [wines] designed to be poured young, are sweet, with low alcohol content, and are a perfect pair for the complex, spicy flavors of Indonesian dishes." Ali's favorite? A sparkling Moscato d'Bali.

The wine world is very small so perhaps it should come as no surprise that I would cross paths with Evy and Mulyati Gozali at some point, but who would have guessed that it would be at a wine tourism conference in Tbilisi, Georgia? Meeting them in person was wonderful and to make it even better they brought along a bottle of that Moscato d'Bali for us to taste. It was just as delicious as Ali said—sweet and softly effervescent with pineapple and papaya notes. It did in fact remind me of a Moscato d'Asti or maybe a tropical Fior d'Arancio. What a splendid treat!

MONSOON VALLE

I regret that I didn't pay more attention to the wine when I visited Thailand in 2000, just a few short years after the Asian financial crisis shook that country and its neighbors. I was more interested in visiting friends and experiencing Thailand itself, which is an exercise in sensory overload if ever there was one. Wine made just one brief appearance and I remember the circumstances pretty well, although I didn't connect all the dots at the time.

Thai wine? I was really surprised when I was offered a glass. When did Thailand start making wine and how is that even possible? Our waiter told us that it was a recent innovation, part of the Thai Rak Thai (Thais Love Thais) movement that had developed in response to the financial crisis. Wine grapes and wine itself, he said, were an attempt to raise the economic conditions of rural farmers whose incomes were hard hit in the market collapse. My glass held Thai wine made by Thai farmers for Thai consumers (and visitors like us, too, of course). Local pride, rural development, and self-sufficiency all tied together. How nice! I accepted the story on face value and didn't ask a lot of questions.

I didn't realize that Thai Rak Thai was much more than just an advertising slogan like "I [Heart] New York" or "Virginia Is for Lovers." Thai Rak Thai was the populist political party led by the controversial Thaksin Shinawatra, which came to power in the early 2000s on a platform of aiding rural famers and other victims of the financial crisis. Thai Rak Thai was soon associated with electoral corruption, however. The Thai military seized control of the government in September 2006 and a tribunal dissolved the party in 2007.

I don't really know if the story our waiter told that night was true—was my wine really part of this political saga? But if it was I remained oblivious to it and to Thai wine in general for several years. It wasn't until we were in London for an international wine symposium that my interest in Thai wine resurfaced.

We happened to have dinner at an upscale Thai restaurant on Imperial Wharf called Blue Elephant, which also has operations in Bangkok, Phuket, Paris, and Brussels. Scanning the wine list for a pre-dinner drink I jumped at the chance to try a Monsoon Valley rosé from Siam Winery in Thailand. I expected to taste the sweet strawberries that you often get with pink wines from emerging regions, but in fact it was fairly dry and very enjoyable. What a surprise. So we ordered a bottle of the Monsoon Bay white wine to have with dinner, a blend of Malaga Blanc and Colombard. Malaga Blanc? Not a grape I was familiar with. But the wine was just right. Light and delicate but, much like the Sababay wine from Bali, a perfect foil to the cuisine. Monsoon Bay? Malaga Blanc? Obviously there was a lot that I needed to learn about New Latitude wines from Thailand. And the story I uncovered is even more surprising than the wines themselves.

The grape is the easiest to explain but possibly most unlikely element of this story. Malaga Blanc is Thailand's most common wine grape, according to *Wine Grapes*, the definitive reference.[4] It is a table grape from the South of France. Louis XIV gave some Malaga Blanc vines to Siam's King Narai the Great in 1685. It thrived in Thailand for fresh consumption and eventual wine production. Malaga Blanc's thick skin helps protect the grapes from heavy monsoon rains. One of the places you will find Malaga Blanc is in the famous floating vineyards of Chao Phraya Delta (the vines grow on pergola structures elevated above small canals). You may not have heard of Malaga Blanc, but it is a grape with a long and rich history.

The history of Siam Winery and Monsoon Valley wine is equally unexpected. Would you believe me if I told you that Siam Winery is a creation of the cofounder of Red Bull, the company that makes the famous energy drink? It's true. The original formula for Red Bull was created by Thailand's Chalerm Yoovidhya, who was running his own small pharmaceutical company when he came up with the idea of this drink and started to market it in 1975. His logo depicted two large red wild gaur (also called Indian bison) charging at each other. The Austrian entrepreneur Dietrich Mateschitz sampled the drink on a trip to Thailand and, convinced that it cured his jet lag, proposed a joint venture. They launched the Red Bull export brand in 1987 and the rest is history. Both men became fabulously rich and the Red Bull name and logo are now ubiquitous.

Apparently not satisfied with his Red Bull success, Chalerm Yoovidhya founded Siam Winery in 1986 and it is now Thailand's largest wine producer. The winery's early growth was fueled by production of a popular wine cooler brand called Spy, a low-alcohol fizzy drink that is still the market leader. Monsoon Valley was launched in 2002 (after my 2000 visit and therefore not the alleged "Thai Rak Thai" wine I was served). About half the 350,000-bottle annual wine production is exported, including the wines we sampled at Blue Elephant in London. Chalerm Yoovidhya died in 2012, but his legacy continues in many ways, including Monsoon Valley wine.

I never would have guessed that a glass of wine could connect Louis XIV to Red Bull or that it would come from floating vineyards in Thailand. Amazing!

THE MONDAVI OF MUMBAI

Phileas Fogg and Passepartout arrived in Bombay from Cairo by a far more direct route than we have taken and then set off on what was planned to be a simple and direct train journey for Calcutta. Their carefully calculated itinerary was crumpled when it turned out that the railroad across the subcontinent had not been completed, as they had been led to believe, and an inconvenient and unexpected gap remained. There followed an improvised adventure that included elephant rides and a moment of high drama when Passepartout demonstrated a previously unimagined courageous side as he rescued a young

Indian woman named Aouda from a group of zealots who were determined to burn her alive.

Much has changed in India since Fogg's days there. Bombay is now Mumbai and Calcutta is Kolkata and of course we are seeking wine, not a fast train. But, as you will see, transportation and cultural differences will be important to us, too.[5]

Persian conquerors brought grapevines to India nearly 2,500 years ago; wine consumption is first mentioned in a text on statecraft written about 300 B.C. Wine was a beverage for elites, not the masses (who apparently wanted stronger stuff), and lived a shadowy existence that continues today due to concerns about alcohol consumption. The influence of British colonizers contributed to the growth of Indian wine production in the nineteenth century, before the scourge of phylloxera hit India's vineyards in the 1890s with predictable results.

Since independence in 1947, wine has been caught in a cross fire in India. On one hand, it is a heavily controlled substance. Article 47 of the constitution makes it a function of the state to discourage alcohol consumption (Gandhi and some other early leaders were teetotalers), so wine imports have always been highly taxed and advertising is forbidden. Individual state governments within India tax and regulate wine sales much as in the United States, creating a distributional crazy quilt. At the same time, however, some state governments promote viticulture and winemaking as an economic development tool. It's a push and shove situation for wine.

The surprising state of wine in India today reflects this complicated condition. On one hand wine is highly taxed and the national market fragmented by uncoordinated state regulatory regimes. The lack of efficient domestic transport limits the market for wine—the wine can be in good shape when it leaves the warehouse, but how will it taste by the time it reaches the consumer? At the same time, pro-development government policies led to an overexpansion of supply by encouraging new vineyard plantings and a subsequent collapse of the industry and consolidation among producers. One winery has emerged from this turmoil in a strong position. It dominates the market with about 60 to 65 percent of sales of Indian wine and it is redefining wine and the wine industry in India. It is called Sula Vineyards.

An article in the Stanford University alumni magazine called Rajeev Samant the "Mondavi of Mumbai" and the title is not much of an overstatement.

Mondavi, also a Stanford graduate, founded the first new winery in Napa Valley since Prohibition, but he didn't just make wine; he helped create a lasting wine culture and wine tourism industry. Samant seems determined to do the same thing in India.[6]

A city kid, Samant went to California to study economics and industrial engineering at Stanford. He worked briefly in Silicon Valley's technology industry before returning home to Mumbai where he sought out an appropriate business opportunity and challenge. You might think that he would be drawn to Bangalore with its many tech startups, but it was Nashik, a rural farming area and pilgrimage destination about 180 kilometers from Mumbai, that became the focus. Samant's father took him to Nashik to see some farmland the family owned and was looking to sell because it wasn't making much of a return.

Samant asked to be given a chance to turn the farm around. He tried mangoes and then table grapes (Sultana grapes, which we call Thompson Seedless in the United States). Both crops were successful in terms of the crop yields, I suppose, but the economic realities are that returns can be limited selling bulk commodities. Not easy to create extra value or to profit from product differentiation with products like these. Then came the "light bulb" moment. If table grapes can grow in Nashik, why not wine grapes?[7] Why not indeed, with the help of California "flying winemaker" consultant Kerry Damskey, who met with Samant in Sonoma and sent him home with India's first Zinfandel cuttings. The vineyard plantings were successful, although, since this was a New Latitudes project, special practices were necessary to deal with temperature, humidity, and the monsoon rains. The fact that Nashik sits at about two thousand feet above sea level is a plus. The first harvest came in 1999 and the winery soon became known for India's first Sauvignon Blanc and Chenin Blanc wines.

Sula Vineyards (named for Samant's mother) helped to create a whole regional wine industry cluster. There are now a few dozen wineries that grow their own grapes and purchase from independent farmers. A modest but growing wine tourism industry has also developed. Sula is at the forefront of the wine, culture, and hospitality strategy that many associate with Robert Mondavi's Napa Valley success. In addition to the winery, which features India's first dedicated tasting room, attracting almost 250,000 visitors in 2016, there are two restaurants, a spa, and as of 2017, India's first heritage wine resort. Sulafest, which is billed as India's largest two-day "gourmet world music" festival, takes places in an amphitheater event space. Sumant has also expanded the business to include Sula Selections, the import part of the operation, which represents iconic wine and spirits brands from around the world. Really, it is an alcoholic United Nations! Adding these imported products to the mix helps the distribution network achieve economies of scale and opens doors for the Sula line. Artisan Spirits, a Sula subsidiary, makes Janus, India's first 100 percent premium grape brandy. A Sula brand of pure grapeseed oil is also produced.

These efforts have been greeted with international praise.[8] Sula received the *Drinks Business* award for Best Contribution to Wine & Spirits Tourism at the 2016 London Wine Fair, for example. And the May 2016 issue of *Wine Enthusiast* magazine gave the 2014 Sula Dindori Reserve Shiraz a score of 92 points and an "Editor's Choice" rating. We found that wine, from the estate vineyard, to have balance and character. But the biggest surprise might have been the Sauvignon Blanc, which had a style of its own—not New Zealand or France or California, either. It takes a bit of courage to make a distinctive wine in a "me, too" world. I like Sula's style!

All in all Sula is an impressive enterprise and the wines have found a growing market both in India and abroad, where they are often featured on Indian restaurant lists. Growing grapes and making wine is always a challenge, especially in new territory such as Nashik, but Samant's real challenge is to help grow the market and culture of wine by defining wine as a "social glue" rather than just another alcoholic beverage. Sula has survived years of poor weather and tumultuous economic conditions to become India's dominant winemaker. There are many challenges ahead, but the Mondavi of Mumbai and his team seem well prepared to handle them.

WHAT'S NEW?

Bali to Thailand to India: what have we learned? As I said at the start, the obvious thread that runs through this part of our journey is about the geography. The New Latitudes proponents challenge conventional wisdom and teach us that it is possible to make not just wine but very good wine in seemingly difficult environments. This is as much a lesson about personal determination as it is about tropical climates, however, and it brings us back to the question that launched this journey: Why wine? What is it about wine that drives people to go to such lengths to grow the grapes, make the wine, and work to create a wine-loving culture? It is clear from this chapter and those that have come before that there is no single simple answer. Wine fills your glass, but it can also fill your heart and focus your mind, inspiring unexpected endeavors like the ones we have seen here.

The New Latitude movement has transformed not just the idea of where and how wine can be produced, but also in many different ways both big and small it has altered the cultural and economic foundations of the societies I've discussed here. Most important, however, is the way that these wines cause those of us who are thoroughly soaked in the conventional wisdom to lift our heads and open our eyes. The world of wine is changing! It's time to change *our* attitudes as well. This is important both in general, I believe, but especially at this point in the book because I need you the reader to have open eyes and an open mind as we take our next step.

⌇

The Wines

Sababay Moscato d'Bali, Indonesia

Monsoon Valley Malaga Blanc/Colombard, Thailand

Sula Dindori Reserve Shiraz, Nashik, India and Sula Sauvignon Blanc, Nashik, India

⌇

Part III
HIGH AND LOW

Chapter 9

Shangri-La

Hugh Conway didn't intend to go to Shangri-La when he threw himself aboard the small twin-engine airplane, a specially equipped model owned by the Maharajah of Chandrapore. He and his three fellow passengers simply sought escape from Baskul, where there was open revolt against the British Raj. But instead of heading for Peshawar and presumed safety, Conway's airplane flew deep into the high Himalayas where, after hours in the air and no communication from the pilot, they ran out of fuel and glided to a crash landing in a remote valley, which Conway reckoned was probably somewhere in Tibet.

They have in fact (or rather in fiction) arrived at Shangri-La, the setting of James Hilton's best-selling 1933 novel, *Lost Horizon*.[1] They are taken to a fabulous lamasery where they are invited to live in luxury and to make use of the libraries of books and music that have been collected here. How all these European objects came to be in this remote place is not entirely clear and the why of it is not obvious, either.

Eventually Conway is introduced to the architect of Shangri-La, a French-speaking Catholic monk named Perrault, who is the High Lama of Shangri-La. He is more than 250 years old. One of the many mysteries of Shangri-La is that some of its residents live far beyond the normal human span. But age is slowed only so long as they remain in the valley. Once they leave, their true tally of years quickly and fatally catches up.

Lost Horizon provides much romance and adventure, which made the 1937 Frank Capra film starring Ronald Coleman and Jane Wyatt such a hit. But it has a serious side, too, which makes you ask questions. Why, I wonder, are Europeans in the book placed on a pedestal? The natives seem more than happy to be exploited and even to die to give the foreign guests the best of everything. And why must Shangri-La itself die or seem to die when the French-speaking High Lama ceases to exist? I don't think anyone would set out to write a novel like this today, where civilization rests so squarely on European shoulders and indigenous peoples are so easily subordinated.

Lost Horizon is very interesting, but what does it have to do with wine? I thought this adventure was supposed to be about wine and inspired by Jules Verne's Phileas Fogg, not James Hilton's Hugh Conway? So here is the connection. Our next stop is a valley high up in the mountains where grapes are grown and, at the behest of a French-speaking leader, fine European-style wine is made to tantalize the palates of global elites. The region is called Shangri-La and, while the wine is very real, whether the place itself is fact or fiction is . . . well, I will leave that up to you. Intrigued? Read on.

WELCOME TO SHANGRI-LA

Tony Jordan wasn't looking for Shangri-La when he came to China in 2009.[2] He was sent by Möet Hennessy, the wine and spirits division of French luxury goods giant LVMH, to find the best place to make a first class Chinese Bordeaux-style wine.[3] The Chinese love Bordeaux, the logic went, and eventually they will produce their own. It only made sense for the French to be the ones to make it.

Cizhong, a tiny village in Yunnan on the banks of the Mekong River along the road to Lhasa in Tibet, was one possibility. French Catholic priest missionaries founded a church more than 150 years ago and planted grapes for sacramental wine and local farmers followed suit. The Communist government sent the missionaries packing in 1952, but the vineyards, tended by local growers, and the wines, too, remained and can be tasted now. French Catholic priests? This sounds a little like the *Lost Horizon* storyline, but there was no magic in the place or secret longevity in the wine. Jordan judged the spot too humid for a top quality vineyard due to the river's influence. And so, guided by climate studies, he went up further along the road toward Lhasa until he came to . . . *Shangri-La!*

Yes, it really was Shangri-La. Or was it? Shangri-La was until 2001 called Zhongdian or Jiantang in Tibetan. Zhongdian made its living from forestry, but the timber industry was in decline and town officials cast about for another source of income. Tourism was the choice and the region had much to offer with the natural beauty of nearby Pudacuo National Park and the cultural pull of the imposing three-hundred-year-old Ganden Sumtsenling Tibetan Buddhist monastery (which actually looks a bit like the *Lost Horizon* Shangri-La monastery of the 1937 film). But would these attractions be enough to draw flocks of tourists to this remove place, ten thousand feet up in mountains? Yes, they decided, if we can just change the name.

And so on December 17, 2001, Zhongdian became Shangri-La and the name change apparently did the job because the tourist industry has indeed blossomed. And then the French came, too, following Tony Jordan's directions, establishing Möet Hennessy Shangri-La (Dequin) Winery and in 2015 releasing the first vintage of their signature wine Ao Yun ("Proud Clouds").

I will confess that all of this made me very nervous when I first read about it. Not the name change to Shangri-La—that's a bit of hype, and I think everyone sees it for what it is. No, it's the French influence that worried me because I flashed back to *Lost Horizon* and my concerns about that book's story, which seemed to privilege all things European over local indigenous people and their culture. Would this real (if not entirely authentic) situation be the same?

I am concerned about what you might call the Shangri-La effect, which can be stated in the form of a simple question. Who benefits from the Chinese wine industry's growth? Outsiders—the French producers and consultants? The multinational merchants and auction houses who are in a position to exploit Chinese wine enthusiasts? Or do the Chinese themselves benefit, Chinese producers, consumers, and merchants? James Hilton's fictional Shangri-La seemed to be organized to benefit the outsiders. Is Chinese wine, including of course its own Shangri-La, the same? That would be a particularly distasteful answer to the "why wine?" question. Why wine? Because it works and the Chinese can't resist it!

THIRSTY DRAGON'S RED OBSESSION

I am not the only one to be worried about China's wine industry and its possibly unhealthy relationship with France. Early reports of French wine sales in China often focused on the gullibility of Chinese buyers, who were easily tricked, it was said, into paying top prices for lesser wines, lesser vintages, and outright fakes. Good news for Bordeaux producers with too much wine and for devious forgers with fraudulent labels. The problem of fakes remains, but much else has changed, as a 2013 documentary film makes clear.

Red Obsession swept the independent film festival circuit winning medals, getting attention, and, for most viewers, introducing a world of Chinese wine that they had not previously imagined.[4] The title is a play on words. Chinese wine drinkers ("red" because of the Communist government) are said to be obsessed with red wine for its health benefits, a preference encouraged by the government at one point in order to promote grape-based wine as an alternative to rice-based alcoholic beverages. And "red" Chinese wine drinkers' great obsessions, for those who can afford them, are the great red wines of France and especially Bordeaux.

Red Obsession painted a picture of a huge nation in the process of going absolutely mad for French wine, bidding up auction prices, drinking up scarce supplies, and taking the next step of buying up the French châteaux themselves. But whereas I am anxious about the Chinese side of this relationship, the film seemed more concerned with the French and global wine generally. Would the Chinese buy up all the great wines? And then all the great wineries? Can nothing be done to stop China from taking over the wine world? An interesting turn of the table.

Times can change quickly and the Chinese threat was changing even before *Red Obsession* was released. No, the Chinese did not lose interest in wine, as we will see in the next few pages, but their particular obsessions changed. A comprehensive government anticorruption crackdown caught ultraexpensive wine sales in its net. Suddenly no one really wanted to be seen giving a bottle of Château Lafite to a high official or accepting a bottle of Château Petrus from a potential supplicant or ordering a bottle of Château Latour at a fancy restaurant. Someone was bound to snap a mobile-phone photo of the occasion to be posted on social media and soon there would be an unfriendly knock on the door from anticorruption agents. Better to avoid these wines altogether than risk investigation.

I have no idea how much of the red obsession was driven by corrupt practices, but the bottom suddenly dropped out of the luxury drinks market in China. The impact was sufficient to be felt in the global accounts of multinational wine firms with strong Chinese sales. Auction prices of the best Bordeaux wines skidded lower, too.

Bordeaux wasn't the only wine region affected, but the impact was perhaps the largest there because predictions of an infinite demand for Bordeaux wines turned out to be wrong. It seems that even very wealthy Chinese investors who purchase for personal satisfaction and not to give as bribes can reach a point where they have all the Château Mouton Rothschild that they desire. Markets turned to Burgundy, the top wines of Italy and Napa Valley, and so on.

Suzanne Mustacich's 2015 book *Thirsty Dragon China's Lust for Bordeaux and the Threat to the World's Best Wines* updated the story. In broad terms, you might say that *Thirsty Dragon* is a love story. First China discovers that it loves Bordeaux, then Bordeaux realizes that it desperately needs China whether it loves her or not, then finally China realizes that its lust for Bordeaux might have been a mistake. In the end we have Chinese-owned Bordeaux châteaux and French investments in China and, in a funny way, it is hard to know where one set of influences and dependencies stops and another begins. Bordeaux may never be the same after its China fling and China has changed a lot, too.

The subtitle suggests a "threat to the world's best wines" and I struggled just a bit trying to decide what Mustacich meant by this. Is the threat due to fraud and counterfeit, which are analyzed in detail here? Is the threat the potential collapse of Bordeaux's *en primeur* system? Or is it the rapidly growing Chinese wine industry itself, with its peculiar characteristics? Certainly Bordeaux has reason to feel threatened by changing economic circumstances, but it is not clear who is to blame for that! Sometimes, as Pogo said, "We have met the enemy and he is us." Clearly the question of who benefits from the rise (or fall) of wine in China is a complicated one.

COLD COMFORT IN NINGXIA

When Tony Jordan was searching for the best place for LVMH to make red wines he was also on the lookout for a sparkling wine outpost and he found it Ningxia. Ningxia is not the most remote wine region in China, but it is close.[5] It is the extremes of temperature that usually draw the first ooohs and aaahs here. At an elevation of more than three thousand feet, Ningxia has long, hot days in the summer and cold, cold nights in the winter. So cold, in fact, that they can be lethal to grapevines, which are typically buried in dirt in the fall to give them a protective blanket and dug out again in the spring.[6]

The Ningxia Agricultural Reclamation Management Bureau did not have many options in the late 1990s when it set out to try to develop a farming industry in the region. Poor soils, extreme temperatures, and unreliable eight-hundred-year-old irrigation canals made for poor prospects. But there was one winery in operation called Xi Xia King. Founded as a cooperative in 1982 and now owned by the local government, it is the region's largest winegrower. Wine grapes require special treatment, but they do very well in poor, rocky soil. So, after some serious investigation, the local government agency decided to go all-in on wine grapes and winemaking. "I've never been anywhere where the local government is so pro wine as the small province of Ningxia," British wine critic Jancis Robinson wrote after her 2012 visit to the region.

Now there are more than fifty wineries in the Ningxia region and the vine-yard landscape has grown to more than eighty thousand acres with plans to double that amount in the next ten years. (California's Napa Valley has about forty-five thousand acres planted to vine.) Ningxia gets a lot of attention from the international press, with Möet Hennessy's $28 million joint venture with a Chinese winery getting much of the ink.

The opening of Möet's big winery in Ningxia in 2013 gave the region the credibility it was seeking and led to the blossoming of wine here. Well, that's the way the story would be told in a Shangri-La world, where outsider atten-tion is the key. But that's not exactly the way the tale developed. Against all odds, the wineries that really paved the way were more Chinese than French. Emma Gao, who was born in Ningxia, studied winemaking in Bordeaux, but her family's Silver Heights winery is very much a Chinese creation and it was in part the quality of her wines that drew international attention to the region. The winery itself is no million dollar showpiece—Jancis Robinson describes it as little more than a collection of sheds on the family's suburban allotment— but the wine that is produced there is rather special.

Ningxia, then, is a region to ponder in the context of this chapter. The drive to create a wine industry here is clearly local, rooted in regional eco-nomic development administration, and driven by local talent, concerns, and interests. The international element cannot be ignored, especially LVMH's sparkling wine investment and Pernod Ricard's success with its Helan Mountain winery, but they are not the whole story, either.

A CITY OF WINE

Would you be surprised to learn that Chinese Riesling and rosé wines won medals at the Panama-Pacific International Exhibition of 1915? The wines were made by Changyu Pioneer Wine Company, which was founded in 1892 by Zhang (Chang) Bishi, a rich overseas Chinese businessman who saw a business opportunity for grape wine in China, especially sales to the large European expat population. He brought *Vitis vinifera* grapevines from Europe to Yantai on the Shandong Peninsula that juts out into the Yellow Sea about four hundred miles southeast of Beijing. It was an ambitious project with large vineyards and a vast underground cellar that took eleven years to complete. Dr. Sun Yat-sen visited the winery in 1912, according to the company website, and pronounced the wines excellent.[7]

Changyu is on the move today, expanding production in China and acquiring producers in other countries. Its signature investment is a huge International City of Wine a few miles from the newly rebranded Yantai Wine Bay resort area. The International City of Wine, which opened in 2016, is intended to be a prime destination for Chinese and Asian tourists, who will come to sniff, swirl, and presumably spend on wine, spirits, and all manner of other things. Among the attractions are an industrial wine production facility, an elaborate museum, and even a European-style village. Changyu seems intent to make this the greatest wine-tourism attraction in the world and, given what I have heard about Chinese wine tourism headcounts, this is not a ridiculous goal.

The Changyu investment is not a solo affair. The regional master plan calls for tens of thousands of acres of vineyard development, billions of dollars of investment, and hundreds of new winery "châteaux." Seriously, if only half the planned investments are completed as planned, this will be the most happening place in the world of wine.

One of the attractions is Great Wall Winery's Château Junding, a $580 million facility with winery, hotel, restaurant, wine village, and 1,700 acres of vines. Great Wall and Changyu are the two largest wineries in China. Great Wall is owned by the romantically named state-owned COFCO, China National

Cereals, Oils and Foodstuffs Corporation. COFCO is known in all its business for secure and efficient supply chains and strong market positioning. Wine is no different with a string of production facilities in China itself plus foreign investments. COFCO was the first Chinese firm to purchase a Bordeaux châ- teau and has added other investments in France, Chile, Australia, and soon perhaps the United States. How important is COFCO? In *Decanter* magazine's 2013 wine-industry "Power List," Wu Fei, the head of COFCO's wine and spirits division, was ranked number two in the world in terms of influence. Only the head of Pernod Ricard, the French drinks group, rated higher and that rank was based in part of the company's success in Asia.

A visit to Yantai offers a very un-Shangri-La experience. Although many of the trappings and much of the architecture are faux-European, this seems to be wine of China, by Chinese and for Chinese. Concerns about dominat- ing European influence are easy to ignore, although closer inspection shows that the China side of things is not the only side. Changyu's success, for example, is due in part to its successful partnership with the French firm Castel. And local wine prestige was enhanced when the Chinese outpost of Château Lafite was opened in Shandong (right next door to Treaty Port, a fanciful winery built to look like a Scottish castle by the financier from Yorkshire who dreamed it up).

Yantai is not the pure Chinese wine scene that I had hoped to find, but it is far from the European-dominated situation that I feared. It's a mix of things, like so much in this interconnected globe, dancing to its own beat and evolv- ing toward . . . who knows what?

RETURN TO SHANGRI-LA

Returning to Shangri-La is a shock after Ningxia and especially Yantai with their big names and huge investments. When my colleagues Pierre Ly and Cynthia Howson visited Shangri-La in 2015 there were no fancy wine cellars, luxury hotels, or corporate PR people to show them around. In fact, Cynthia told me, she had to revert to the techniques she used when doing disserta- tion research about women smugglers in Senegal. I call it "commando field- work," although I am sure there is a better technical term. It involves meeting people, getting their trust, moving from connection to connection, personal network to personal network, village to village, until finally (or in some cases not) meeting the person you need to meet and learning something important. Cynthia's well-developed grassroots networking instincts guided them through the string of little villages that make up the Shangri-La vineyard area until at last, with the light fading, they knocked on an unmarked guesthouse door and saw in the glowing light within a familiar collection of faces from China, France, Argentina, and more. Pay dirt! They had entered Shangri-La through the back door!

Although the Shangri-La winery was famous around the world because of the LVMH luxury multinational connection even before it released its first wine, the reality is that the operations are in many ways a very local thing. The vineyards are small and owned by local peasants who are used to tending their vines for quantity rather than quality. Changing their mindset has not been easy. Nor apparently was it very easy to get a modern winery built, according to LVMH wine chief Jean-Guillaume Prats. A great deal of excess capacity was built into the cellar operation because of the unlikelihood of ever getting a construction crew, equipment, materials, and so on into the area again. Shangri-La has the highest production cost of any wine in the LVMH portfolio—even higher than Chateau d'Yquem. When I met Prats at a conference in London he kind of shrugged when talking about Shangri-La, suggesting that maybe we are not meant to produce wines, even very good wines, everywhere in the world just because we can.[8]

Shangri-La is not an easy project and it is not entirely a French one. The local government, which originally created the opportunity by encouraging grape farming, struck a deal with VATS Group, formerly the Jinliufu Liquor Company, a Chinese spirits producer (baijiu, a traditional Chinese liquor, is their thing—they have fifteen distilleries) to make wine. VATS Liquor Chain is China's largest group of liquor outlets. It's quite a dynamic company and so it perhaps makes sense that it is LVMH's partner in the Shangri-La project.

WHICH WINES?

The wines for this part of the journey must necessarily include the Shangri-La Winery Ao Yun 2013, a blend of Cabernet Sauvignon with a little Merlot, even though neither Pierre, Cynthia, nor I have tasted it and at three hundred dollars per bottle it will take a while to save up to buy it. But how can I resist a wine from Shangri-La?

I asked Pierre and Cynthia to choose the rest of the wines because of their superior knowledge of China and its wines (they are writing a book about the industry). Their list begins with the wine that put China and Ningxia on the world map for many skeptical experts. Helan Qing Xue's Jiabeilan 2009 Cabernet blend shocked people when it won the Red Bordeaux Varietal Over £10 International Trophy in the 2011 Decanter World Wine Awards.

Grace Vineyard's 2012 Tasya's Reserve Marselan is next because it represents both one of the leading quality wineries and also the evolution of Chinese wine from a narrow focus on Bordeaux varieties to an appreciation of the wider world of wine. Marselan is a cross between Cabernet Sauvignon and Grenache that was created in the 1960s specifically to expand quality grape options in the Languedoc. Grace is also pushing the Chinese envelope with an Aglianico. Very exciting! Silver Height's Family Reserve is next to represent a different dimension, the struggles of a tiny family winery that reaches for the heights of quality.

The list ends with Domaine Chandon Brut Rosé from Ningxia, the sparkling sister of the Shangri-La red and a tip of the hat to the Sino-French collaboration that both wines represent. It is also a useful reminder that this Shangri-La is not a carbon copy of the one that James Hilton imagined. International actors and influences are important to wine here and will be for many years, but the momentum has shifted and local forces are becoming dominant. Is the idea of distinctly Chinese wine industry and culture a "Lost Horizon?" I think not.

~

The Wines

Shangri-La Winery Ao Yun 2013, China

Helan Qing Xue's Jiabeilan Cabernet blend 2009, China

Grace Vineyard Tasya's Reserve Marselan 2012, China

Silver Heights Family Reserve, China

Domaine Chandon (Ningxia) Brut Rosé, China

~

Chapter 10

Australia

The Library and the Museum

"Savour Australia" was organized to relaunch Brand Australia on the world wine stage. Somehow Australia had become known for a certain style of simple, inexpensive wine (especially Shiraz and Chardonnay) and Savour Australia's goal was to let everyone know that Aussie wine has much more to offer (which it does). The event was an exercise in sensory overload, with people from all over the world, the food, the wines, the speeches, and so on. But as our heads cleared on the long flight back home to Seattle, a couple of themes emerged that help us think about Australian wine and about the world of wine more generally. Appropriately they are inspired by two spectacular wine tastings.

AUTHENTICALLY AUSTRALIAN

"Shiraz: The Australian Way" was held in the historic Mortlock Wing of the State Library of South Australia, just up the road from the main conference venue. Think dark wood, musty old book smells, and a single long table filled with wineglasses. There, a small group of us spent the afternoon thinking, talking, and, well, even drinking Australian Shiraz. If the goal was to make us understand that Aussie Shiraz is not just a jammy alcoholic fruit bomb, it worked.

The first tasting flight presented glasses filled with Shiraz from many different Australian regions, so that we could begin to appreciate the complexity of Aussie *terroir*. One of Australia's strategies, which many other wine regions are also pursuing, is to focus on the diversity of *terroirs* in order to elevate and differentiate its quality wines and disassociate them from simple supermarket products.

Terroir is a hot marketing concept these days because it is seen as an indicator of authenticity. Consumers are now familiar with the concept of *terroir* generally, eating oysters from specific beaches, drinking single-estate coffees and teas, munching single-estate chocolate. One big spirits company even released a single-estate vodka, which confused me quite a bit. I am not a vodka drinker, but as I understand it vodka is defined as colorless, odorless, and tasteless. If that's true, then this special vodka must be noteworthy because it isn't sensually neutral in general, but somehow captures the particular sensual emptiness of a particular place. Who knew that was even possible? Amazing. (Perhaps it has a distinctive texture?)

The wines, all from the 2009 and 2010 vintages, told their regional stories very well. Plantagenet, De Bortoli, Jamsheed, Jasper Hill, McWilliams, d'Arenberg, Spinifex, and Torbreck. If you know Australian wines, you appreciate that we were in good hands. Time was called and we were sent off to roam around the library and snack on cheeses and cured meats while the wineglasses were cleared away and replaced, then filled so that the second act could begin.

This group of wines was meant to demonstrate how Australian Shiraz develops over time, so we tasted wines from 1996, 1997, 1998, 1999, 2004, and 2005 and names like Craiglee, Best "Bin O," Mount Langi Ghiran, Rockford Basket Press, Jim Barry The Armagh, and Clonakilla. The wines, which came from different places and years and had been made according to different philosophies, presented a fascinating study. Finally, inevitably, a quiet fell as we turned our attention to the last glasses in the flight, two icons of Australian Shiraz: Penfolds Grange and Henschke Hill of Grace. We tasted, savored, and then began to talk. There was a lot to talk about.

Penfolds Grange is arguably Australia's most famous wine. Henschke Hill of Grace is well known to Aussie fine wine fans if less so to wine enthusiasts in general. To taste either one is considered a treat. To taste them both, as we did, is a rare luxury. They are, along with Torbreck's The Laird, typically the most expensive Aussie wines, selling for between five hundred and one thousand dollars per bottle upon release and often much more in the secondary market. While price is obviously not a foolproof indicator of quality by any means, prices like these sure do get your attention.

But the debate at our end of the table wasn't about which wine cost the most or whether any of them were worth their lofty price tags. No, the discussion centered on a far more fundamental question. Which was the truest expression of wine? (I guess drinking fine wine in a musty old library brings out the philosopher in all of us!) Although Grange and Hill of Grace are both great wines, they represent very different ideas of wine, which the stories that are told about them immediately capture. If wine is meant to make a statement, as all of our eighty wines must do to earn their place on our brief list, then what should it say? Let me tell you the two stories and let you decide.

MAX AND CYRIL'S AUDACIOUS IDEA

Max Schubert was the chief winemaker at Penfolds from 1948 to 1975, a period of enormous change in Australian wine for which he was partly responsible.[1] Fortified wines—domestically produced "ports" and "sherries" (we wouldn't call them by these protected names today)—dominated the wine market.[2] The best of these wines were fantastic (as the best Australian fortifieds are today), but they crowded out the development of table wine in the European tradition.[3]

Given these circumstances, Schubert's bosses expected him to march to the tune of the market and produce more and better fortified wine. But a visit to Bordeaux changed his plans and when he returned to Australia he started work on making an Australian wine that could stand alongside the great wines of France. He made the wine in the company cellars in Adelaide starting in 1951 and was finally called to the company's Sydney headquarters in 1957 to present his work to the directors. They tasted and talked and ordered the project . . . terminated! It might have been a fine wine (indeed the 1955 was spectacular, as it later turned out), but it wasn't what the market at that time wanted. Penfolds' website cites a critic who tasted the wine and wrote, "Schubert, I congratulate you. A very good, dry port, which no one in their right mind will buy—let alone drink." Grange (or Penfolds Grange Hermitage as it was known for many years) was dead.

Except it wasn't. The considerable distance between the cellar in Adelaide and the headquarters in Sydney allowed Schubert more autonomy than might otherwise have been the case. He continued to make Grange in secret, blending wines from different vineyards and regions in the search for a truly great wine. When the board was persuaded to revisit the project in 1960, they tasted again and changed their minds. What had changed? Well, Schubert had built the wines to last, so they had changed in a good way. But the Australian market had changed, too, which must have made a difference. Production was "restarted," having never actually been stopped. Penfolds Grange went on to earn honors and awards around the world and to attain the cult-wine status that it continues to enjoy today.

Schubert's vision and stubborn determination are inspiring and the wines have surely earned their iconic status. But they were and are a very particular idea of great wine. The spotlight shines brightest on the chief winemaker himself—Schubert, then Don Ditter, John Duval (whom we met in Adelaide), and now Peter Gago—who creates a different multiregion blend each year to produce a signature wine. The wines come from fine vineyards, to be sure, but it is the skill of the winemaker that is celebrated, usually with reference back to the man who started it all. Thus Robert Geddes MW's review of the 2008 Grange (he gave it 97 points and a drinking window stretching out to 2040) began with the words "Max [Schubert] would be impressed. . . ."[4]

Max Schubert was not the only one thinking that fine table wines, not the more popular fortifieds, were the way forward for Australia in the 1950s. Fourth-generation winemaker Cyril Alfred Henschke also began to shift his winemaking in the European-inspired direction. In 1956 nearly two-thirds of Henschke's wines were fortified, but by 1959 production was 100 percent table wine. How could Henschke move so quickly? One reason is that he did not have to move in secret, hiding his activities from a suspicious board in Sydney. There was no place to hide and no one to hide from. Henschke was (and is) a family winery and Cyril, the fourth generation in his family to make wines in Keyneton near Tanunda in the Barossa Valley, was in charge.[5]

Henschke had a choice to make when crafting his first wines because the family owned several vineyards in Eden Valley (and now also the Adelaide Hills). He could have followed Schubert's model and blended from different areas, but instead he decided to make the vineyard, not the winemaker, the story. The first great wine, released in 1958, was called Henschke Hill of Grace. It is a single-vineyard wine that reflects what that particular site offers each year (except for 1974, 2000, and 2003, when grape quality was poor and no wine was made). Stephen Henschke, Cyril's son and the current winemaker, has stayed the course his father set and Henschke is known today for its single-vineyard wines, including the Mount Edelstone Shiraz and the Julius Riesling.

If you ever get to visit the place you will discover that Hill of Grace vineyard is not on a hill. It sits adjacent to the Gnadenberg Church where the Henschke family has worshiped over the years. Gnadenberg means "hill of grace." The vineyard, which was first planted more than 150 years ago, features gnarled, ancient, dry-farmed Shiraz vines that give up a small but rather spectacular crop each year, which is made into this iconic wine.

Grange speaks to the winemaker's art. Hill of Grace expresses the nature of a particular place. Have you tasted these wines? If you have, I wonder which you prefer (I will reveal my bias at the end of the chapter). If not, then I wonder which idea of wine you would think is more important. All wines are products of both craft and nature, of course, and these two are no different. They reveal a tension that defines wine or at least our understanding of it. I find it interesting that these two wines, made from the same grape variety and first produced at about the same moment but different in so many other ways, should have had such a profound impact on Australian wine history.

THE MUSEUM TASTING

The library tasting of Australian Shiraz, with its Grange versus Hill of Grace finale, was memorable enough to serve as the highlight to any wine lover's week (or month or year, I suppose). But it was matched, if that's possible, by another tasting the very next day, which I will call the museum tasting, although it didn't happen in a museum. This tasting taught us even more about Australian wine's past and future and revealed another fundamental tension in wine today.

Yalumba's proprietor Robert Hill Smith generously invited a few of us to The Old Lion Cellar & Tunnels in Adelaide to take part in a special tasting of museum wines—wines drawn from the Yalumba cellars' collection of older, rarer wines from around the world and across Australia's many *terroirs*. Our meeting, which took place in the atmospheric vaulted cellars beneath The Old Lion, was the twenty-fourth in a series that began in 1977. Initially the focus was internal, I'm told, to let Australia's young winemakers taste some of the very best wines across both time and space and be informed and inspired by them. A sure cure for "cellar palate" complacency. Our tasting was more for export—to allow an international audience to appreciate today's fine Australian wines in historical context.

The oldest wine was a 1922 fortified Shiraz "port," but nearly as old was a Yalumba Riesling from 1938. Riesling? We think of Australia as a British colony, but many of the early settlers to the Barossa Valley came from Silesia, then part of Germany and now mostly in Poland. That's where the Henschke family came from when they first arrived here in 1841. No surprise that these immigrants would seek cool spots to plant Riesling vines.

The Yalumba tasting, which included wines from Vasse Felix, Jim Barry, and Henschke, was the ultimate personal experience—a conversation where the wines literally speak for themselves, telling stories of the past and present with implications for the future, even as we tasters talked about what we were discovering. Interestingly, one of the stories the wines told was about family, since they were all the products of multigeneration family wine businesses like Henschke and Yalumba, which is Australia's oldest family winery dating from 1847. Old wine is one thing, but old wineries are another. The fact that family wineries could last so long is amazing given the wild ride they have been through.[6] The fact that they would after all this time be recognized as national icons demands explanation. Is it a coincidence that family is so important in the world of wine?

WHY FAMILY WINERIES ARE UNEXPECTEDLY IMPORTANT

The featured essay in the November 1, 2014, issue of *The Economist* newspaper focused on family businesses and made the case that they are a surprisingly robust feature of postindustrial capitalism. The conventional wisdom, as *The Economist* explains, is that family businesses were a natural fit with early capitalism, when trust was at a premium and finance mainly came from within the family or the firm itself.[7] There are problems with family firms, however, which are said to limit their scale, scope, and longevity. The British have a saying that it is "clogs to clogs in three generations" as the dynamism that built the family firm is dissipated and the business eventually shrinks, fails, or falls into the hands of outsiders.[8] The conventional wisdom, descended from management guru Alfred Chandler and others, is that the modern company is increasingly rationalized and best run by highly trained hired professional managers, not hereditary top dogs. The irrational, unprofessional family necessarily plays a smaller and smaller role.

The family-ownership structure is supposed to limit access to capital and make expansion and effective management difficult. And yet many of the most famous names in the wine industry are family-owned firms. Some, like the Gallos of California and the Ruperts of South Africa, have kept ownership closely held for years. Others, like the Antinoris of Italy, have experimented with outside capital only to return, at considerable expense, to the family model. *The Economist* article cites Berry Bros. & Rudd, the London fine-wine merchant that serves as the start and finish line for this book. The discussion of BB&R focuses on the ability of families to ride out short term crises while keeping an eye on the horizon. Once your business has lived through the South Sea Bubble, seventh-generation company chief Simon Berry quips, you are ready for whatever the modern economy throws at you.

Why are family-owned wineries so vibrant despite their structural economic limitations? The conventional answer to this question—and there is in fact a substantial academic literature dealing with family businesses and even family wine businesses—stresses the ways that family businesses take a multigenerational approach and are able to negotiate the trade-off between short-run returns and long-run value. Corporations, it is said, are sometimes driven too much by quarterly returns and end up sacrificing long term interests to achieve immediate financial goals. When business requires a long-run vision, it is said, families gain an advantage. Wine is certainly a business where it is necessary to look into the future if only because vines are perennials, not annuals like corn or soybeans, and successful brands aspire to be perennials, too.

But maybe the question isn't why family-owned wine businesses are so robust and instead why corporate-owned wine businesses are sometimes so fragile. Is there something about wine that turns smart corporate brains to mush (not all of them, of course, but maybe some of them)? One difference that I have noticed about family wine businesses versus some of the corporations regards the role of key assets such as brand and reputation. Many family wineries that come to mind seem to see their role as *protecting* brand and reputation so that they will continue to provide benefits well into the future. Some corporations that come to mind, on the other hand, seem to focus on *leveraging* brand and reputation in order to increase short run returns.

What's the problem with leveraging a brand? Leverage has the potential to increase returns in any business, but it also increases risk. And one risk is that the integrity of key assets can be undermined by the leverage process itself. An example? Well, I hate to pick on Treasury Wine Estates, which is based here in Australia, but one of my readers e-mailed me in dismay when a news story appeared about a Treasury market strategy. I'll use this as an example, but Treasury isn't the only wine corporation that I could pick on and is maybe not even the best example.[9]

One element of Treasury's plan was to develop brands for the "masstige" market segment, which means taking a prestige brand and leveraging it by introducing a cheaper mass-market product that rides on the iconic brand's reputation. Masstige? Sounds like something from a Dilbert cartoon, which means of course that it is a totally authentic contemporary business term. Prestige fashion house Versace, for example, seems to have developed a very successful masstige product line for mass-market retailer H&M. If masstige worked for shoes and dresses, how could it be a bad idea for wine?

I'm sure a prestige association helps sell the cheaper mass-market products, but I can think of some examples in the wine business where it might have undermined the iconic brand itself a little (Beringer White Zinfandel) or a lot (Paul Masson, once California's most expensive wine), which seems self-defeating. I know that has happened in the fashion field (think about how the Pierre Cardin brand was diluted by cheap logo products), so I imagine it could be a factor in wine, too.

Here's another example. Regional identity is more important in wine than in some other industries and Treasury owns some famous "wine of origin" brands—wines associated with particular regions, which are valuable assets. But my worried reader was concerned about Treasury's plan to source globally to expand the scale of some of these regional brands.

"Building scale via sourcing breadth is one of the most critical platforms necessary for the globalization of wine brands," according to the report. Gosh, that even sounds like corp-speak, doesn't it? Logical, I suppose, but maybe locally defined brands need to be locally sourced to maintain their integrity? Treasury has no doubt studied this thoroughly and they are probably right about their strategies and I am probably wrong, but it seems problematic to me. I wonder if family firms are more likely to resist corporate wine-think and try to protect key assets like a prestige brand or a regional identification while corporations are driven instead to try to leverage these assets to expand their market share?

CIRCLING BACK TO GRANGE AND HILL OF GRACE

All of which brings us back to Penfolds Grange versus Henschke Hill of Grace and the paradox these two wines present. Both have a long wine industry in Australia and both started as family firms, but where Henschke has weathered the storms in its original family form, Penfolds (as you might have gathered from the Sydney board story) grew bigger and more expansive. In 1990 it was purchased by Southcorp, a company that started its life in Adelaide in 1859 as West End Brewery. West End expanded through acquisitions (economies of scale are very important in brewing) and eventually diversified into wine as well as packaging and, for some reason, the manufacture of water heaters.[10] Eventually Southcorp, with Penfolds, Lindeman's, and Rosemount brands in its portfolio, refocused on wine only to end up being purchased by Foster's, a big Australian beer producer seeking diversification, in 2005.

Foster's experienced economic distress due both to the global financial crisis and the fact that it had purchased Southcorp at the top of the market. Under increasing financial pressure, Foster's eventually split its poor-performing wine assets into a separate company called Treasury Wine Estates, which has made slow but significant progress to rationalize and revitalize its global wine portfolio, of which Penfolds is a shining star. At this writing I am happy to say that Treasury is reporting strong sales and profit growth, which is a good thing since much rides on its success.

Poor Penfolds has been passed from owner to owner in this way as have many other famous wine brands and it is impressive (Max would indeed be proud) that the quality of their wines has survived the double whammy of revolving-door corporate control and the more general cycles and challenges of the Australian wine industry that caused Wine Australia to call us all together at Savour Australia to relaunch its brand on the global stage. I hope Penfolds now can also survive the pressure to leverage its reputation through lower-priced masstige offerings and globally sourced stablemates.

Grange and Hill of Grace are great wines, but more than that they are survivors and they tell us something important about wine, Australia, and perhaps even ourselves. I like them both and admire the bold winemakers who created them, but I cannot deny that I prefer Hill of Grace. Is it the wine? Or is it the idea of wine that it represents?

～

The Wines

Penfolds Grange Bin 95 Shiraz, South Australia, Australia

Henschke Hill of Grace Shiraz, Eden Valley, Australia

～

Chapter 11

Tasmania

Cool Is Hot

Our plane touched down at the Hobart airport and we pointed our rental Kia Sportage toward Richmond, a historic village on the Coal River. One of the town's main attractions is an 1823 bridge built by penal laborers. We passed through town then up a long gravel road before turning up a long dirt-and-gravel driveway leading to Tara's Farmstay, a farm right on the river where the proprietors, two agricultural scientists, raise sheep and cattle, plant row crops, and take in guests like us. They have a few vines, too, and make a little Pinot Noir for their own consumption. Sue loved the chance to feed a tiny lamb that came around one morning. We like to stay with growers and farmers when can, to get a sense of place that is hard to grasp from the lounge of the InterContinental Hotel, as nice as that can be.[1]

Tasmania is an off-the-beaten-path destination. You have to want to come here to get here today, which is ironic since it is so closely associated with its past as a convict settlement. Most of the early residents didn't want to be here at all. Great Britain sent some of its most hardened criminals to serve time at Port Arthur. These days enthusiastic tourists and settlers come to Tasmania for the history (both Port Arthur and the coal mines district are UNESCO World Heritage sites) and the natural beauty. And, oh yes, they come for the wine. Tasmania may not be on your wine radar yet, but it soon will be. It is one of the hottest emerging wine regions on earth.

WINES TO DIE FOR

Tasmania is home to four distinct wine regions, one up north near Devonport, another down the Tamar Valley, a third scattered along the east coast, and the fourth down south near Hobart and Richmond, where we were based. Many noteworthy wines are made on the island—we were particularly impressed by the Freycinet Pinot Noir from the east coast. The Coal River Valley is home to more than fifteen wineries ranging from the humble to the elaborate. Frogmore Creek has a sleek, modern tasting room, for example, and a gourmet restaurant, too. And although they are hardly on the beaten track, Frogmore Creek was sold out of many of their wines when we visited, which suggests that wine tourism is thriving here. The Pinot Noir from Tolpuddle Vineyards, which we were unable to visit during our Coal River Valley excursion, was named one of the eleven best Pinot Noirs in the world outside of Burgundy by *Decanter* magazine's Stephen Brook in 2016.[2] It is a project of Martin Shaw and Michael Hill Smith, who make great wine in the Adelaide Hills but set up shop in Tasmania as well because they couldn't resist the opportunity.

One of my favorite Tasmanian wines comes from a company called Jansz, its name inspired by Abel Janszoon Tasman, who discovered the island that now bears his name in 1642. Jansz makes sparkling wines using the "Méthode Tasmanoise," which is to say the same classic method they use in Champagne. This makes sense since the winery was founded in 1986 as a partnership between a local company and Louis Roederer Champagne. The French saw in Tasmania's Pipers River region of the Tamar Valley the same marginal wine-growing climate as back home in Champagne. Perfect for the sort of high-acid base wines that are used to make great sparkling wines. The Hill Smith family of Yalumba wine fame bought Jansz in 1997.[3] Not too much is exported, Robert Hill Smith tells me. Limited grape supply plus strong Australian demand conspire to restrict foreign sales.

Our main wine destination in the Coal River Valley was Domaine A, whose Cabernet Sauvignon is reputed to be the best such wine in Australia (an audacious claim to be sure) and is featured in the book *1001 Wines You Must Taste Before You Die*.[4] Domaine A is the project of Peter Althaus, a Swiss IBM engineer whose passion for Bordeaux wines drove him to search the world for the perfect site to make this style of wine. He wanted a cool site where he could make wines of exceptional elegance and he finally found what he was looking for in the Coal River Valley. He and his wife purchased and further developed the Stoney Vineyard, the oldest in the region, having been first planted in 1973. The vineyard is well named and the site is compact, but with diverse aspects and notably rocky soil. A thick mist settled over the landscape on the day we visited, giving it an almost eerie atmosphere.

The winemaking is precise, as you would expect of a Swiss engineer. Each of the Domaine A wines is distinctive, with its own personality, and I can't really say which I like the best. Certainly the Pinot Noir was unlike any Pinot I had tasted before, perhaps because Althaus isn't really a fan of Burgundy and so felt free to express his own views. The Lady A Fumé Blanc oaked Sauvignon Blanc was also a stunner. And while I don't want to tempt the Grim Reaper just yet, the Domaine A Cabernet Sauvignon does live up to its *1001 Wines* Bucket List hype. A cult wine from Tasmania. Who would have guessed? Peter Althaus, I guess. Ahead of his time . . . in more ways than one.

WHAT MAKES COOL TASMANIA HOT

Louis Roederer and Peter Althaus came to Tasmania for different reasons and to make different wines, but the cool climate was important in both cases. Marginal climates are best for sparkling wines, for example, because secondary fermentation turns an acidic base wine into the bright, bubbly wine we all love. And Althaus wanted a cool site, where he could just barely ripen his Cabernet Sauvignon grapes, to get a certain balance and refinement that might be lacking elsewhere. To make sparkling wine in Tasmania must have seemed crazy back in the 1980s, but Althaus would have seemed crazier still when bought the Stoney Vineyard in 1990. Ripeness was all the rage then and warmer sites much more prized. But times have changed and both investments now look very smart. Sparkling wines are more popular than ever (spurred by the Prosecco boom) and lower-alcohol, elegant red wines are back in vogue. But neither of these is the reason for the increased attention to winemaking in Tasmania.

Tasmanian cool is hot these days because of climate change, which is making warm regions hot and hot regions hotter. Many believe that as Australia heats up, fine-wine production will shift to Tasmania and other cool locations such as the Mornington Peninsula near Melbourne, the source of another of

Stephen Brook's "best outside Burgundy" Pinot Noir wines. The search is on, in Australia and around the world, for cool-climate winegrowing regions.

COAL MINE CANARY: CLIMATE CHANGE

Climate change's potential impact on the wine you drink and the wine industry that makes it is very important and so I hope you will not object to a brief digression on the subject before we go back to choosing our eighty wines.

It is not ridiculous to think of wine as the "canary in the coal mine" when it comes to climate change and especially to climate warming. Although grapevines are remarkably robust plants, the climate window for specific varieties of wine grapes, *Vitis vinifera*, and especially for high-quality grapes for fine wine, is surprisingly narrow.[5] Viticultural climatologist Professor Gregory V. Jones has studied the situation closely because it is of both personal and professional interest. His family owns Abacela Winery in Roseburg, Oregon, which quite opposite to the perceived wisdom of Oregon as a cool-climate Pinot Noir location, specializes in wines made from Spanish grape varieties.

Jones's research shows that quality grapes can thrive in conditions where average growing season temperatures range between about 13°C to 20°C, which corresponds to a range from a cool average of 55°F to a warmer 68°F (raisins and table grapes do best at the warmer end of this spectrum and are compatible with average temperatures up to 24°C). But the temperature range for specific grape varieties is much narrower. Quality Riesling, for example, prefers average growing season temperatures from about 13°C to 17°C, a relatively wide range compared with Pinot Gris, which does not like a growing environment much above an average temperature of 15°C.

Pinot Noir's range is about 14°C to 16°C and if the temperature rises higher than that a quality wine grape producer needs to start looking at Tempranillo, Dolcetto, or maybe Merlot, all of which can produce grapes from about 16°C to 19°C. If the temperature goes higher still, we are talking about heat-loving Carignan, Zinfandel, and Nebbiolo. The quality wine grape growing window closes shut altogether when average season temperatures rise above about 22°C, according to Jones.

There are climate-change criers and climate-change deniers and the gulf between them seems to cut along more or less political lines. If you are looking for warming trends, you will certainly find them. For example, 2016 was by some measures the globe's warmest year since records were first kept.[6] That year broke the global heat records set in 2015 and 2014. The other top six warmest year records were also set in this century: 2010, 2013, and 2005, in descending order. Indeed, fourteen of the top fifteen hottest years on record occurred in the twenty-first century (the other one was in 1998). The data makes it pretty clear that someone has turned up the global thermostat. But who?

Are rising temperatures caused by human activity (all that coal being burned as China's economy has grown, for example)? Or is it a natural phenomenon, since we know that there have been cycles in the global climate in previous centuries? Or is it simply weather, not climate, an unlucky and possible but improbable string of several randomly warmer years in a row?

I have encountered only a few climate-change deniers in the wine business and perhaps this is because farmers (and that's what winegrowers are) tend to keep very good records of each season's weather so that they can refer back in later years. Clearly the winegrowers in South Australia who are increasingly looking to Tasmania as insurance against climate change see the threat as real. Moving to Tasmania is cool-headed farming logic to them.

THE TIPPING POINT?

And research based upon those detailed farmer records makes it clear that cool-headed thinking is needed. According to Jones's studies, the observed growing season temperature average for wine regions around the world increased by 1.3°C between 1950 and 2000 (put in perspective, that increase is more than half Pinot Noir's ideal temperature range), shifting some regions into the sweet spot for particular wine grape varieties and others toward the upper edge. Indeed, speaking of sweet spots, one of the complications of climate change in wine is that, up until quite recently, the overall impact was probably quite positive for many or even most regions. Higher temperatures, longer growing seasons—these changes might well be seen as pluses not minuses, with riper, fuller wines that suited the prevailing style.

Jones's climate projections, however, suggest that global wine is reaching or perhaps has reached a tipping point. Average growing season temperatures for the same regions are projected to continue to rise significantly, effectively ending long-standing *terroir* associations between specific locations and signature grape varieties in many cases. The Jones family's decision to plant Tempranillo in Southern Oregon looks smarter and smarter with each passing year.

So what is to be done? Well, individual winegrowers can only do so much to halt or reverse global warming itself through direct action, whatever its ultimate human or natural causes might be. (Although many of these winegrowers act as good role models for the rest of us through their adoption of solar power and other conservation practices.) They can't all pack up shop and move to Tasmania, either. But there are a lot of intermediate steps that can be (and are being) taken, starting with shifts to Tempranillo and other grape varieties that do well at higher average temperatures. Some South Australian winegrowers are regrafting their existing rootstocks with more heat-friendly grape varieties that originated in Spain and Southern Italy. They are also looking for more heat-resistant clones of their current grape varieties and experimenting with canopy management techniques to give currently planted grapes more cooling shade. I have also heard of plans to replant vineyards so that the vine rows run east-to-west rather than north-to-south. A north-south vineyard gets morning sun on one side and afternoon sun on the other, with the leafy canopy protecting the grapes from the noon heat. An east-west vineyard, on the other hand, gets some of that canopy protection all day long. Pulling out vines and putting in new varieties . . . or pulling grapes out entirely in favor of other crops . . . these are last-resort measures that were once thought to be far in the distant future. But the future is now, or at least not so far off as we once thought, for some wine regions.

THE ENGLISH WINE BOOM

Tasmania isn't the only small island that is experiencing a climate change–driven wine boom. This journey's starting line and its final destination—England—is also enjoying rapid wine growth. And the wines can be very good. If you run across an English wine, you should try it. Sue and I actually make a point to stop by a restaurant called Plane Food in Terminal 5 whenever we pass through London's Heathrow Airport (it is part of celebrity chef Gordon Ramsay's dining empire) simply because they always have some new English wine for us to try. The current drinks menu as I am writing this includes two sparkling English rosés and a white wine from Kent.

By the way, it is English wine that you want to try, not British wine. What's the difference? Isn't England part of Great Britain? So logically shouldn't English wine be British (along, presumably, with any wines made in Scotland, Wales, and Northern Ireland)? Logic, alas, will only take you so far in the world of regional wine identity. English wine is made in England from fresh grapes grown in England, just as you might have thought. British wine, however, is made in Britain from wine concentrate imported from some other place and restored to its original form by the addition of fine British (I presume) water.

The rapid recent rise of English wine is the result of a combination of geology plus climate change. Climate change is happening in England creating an environment that is no longer off the wine map. Climate change is also happening in France and in particular in the Champagne region, where a marginal climate is warming up and becoming less suited to the making of Champagne. Improving weather, including a longer growing season, does the opposite for Champagne as it has done for other regions such as Bordeaux. The weather is becoming *too* good to make the acidic wines that, once refermented in the bottle to achieve a yeasty fizz, make the best Champagne wines.

The future of Champagne is uncertain as the world warms up. I don't think Champagne will ever go away, although it seems likely that it will change. Others can use the same grape varieties as Champagne and employ the same production techniques, but can they copy the chalky soil that lends a certain something to these wines? Well, the English can't copy the soil, but they don't have to because, at least in some places, they have it already. Think "white cliffs of Dover." Those white cliffs would be made from more or less the same stuff as the Champagne vineyards, a fact that has caught the wine world's attention and accounts for the keen interest in English sparkling wines in particular.

Two-thirds of English wine is sparkling and, while most of the vineyards are small and the projects of people who earned their wealth in other lines of business, the French themselves have planted a flag here as well. Jancis Robinson reports Champagne house Taittinger is engaged in a joint venture in Kent with UK importers Hatch Mansfield. The first vines are set to be planted (in suitable chalky soil) in 2017. How long before English demand for Champagne can be satisfied by local producers? From little vines, a mighty wine industry may grow.[7]

It is difficult to choose which English wine to represent this chapter in the story, but I think I will select Nyetimber in West Sussex, which Robinson credits with starting the modern English sparkling wine movement when they planted their vineyards on chalky soil at a historic (it appears in the 1086 Domesday book) estate. The Nyetimber Classic Cuvée is a modern classic, "one of England's finest sparkling wines," according to Jamie Goode's review in the *Sunday Express*, "this is pretty serious stuff . . . refined and textured, with great balance." High praise. The price is in line with Champagne, too, at a bit over thirty pounds. With 6.3 million bottle total production in 2014, English sparkling wine is already encroaching on the 32.7 million imported Champagne bottles. Who knows where it will end? Powered by chalky soils and climate change, it is easy to imagine exponential growth. But that might be a mistake.

CLIMATE CHANGE GIVES AND IT TAKES AWAY

A mistake? Yes, the problem is that climate change isn't simply global warming, it is also an increase in local weather variability. Think global, but fear local might be a good motto looking into the future. Have you noticed that some of the storms in your area are more frequent or severe than in the past? That the seasons sometime feel a bit out of order? Dry summers become droughts and wet winters hit rainfall record levels. Could be that you have a poor memory, could be random weather events, or it could be something bigger.

A 2016 scientific research paper titled "Impact of recent climate change and weather variability on the viability of UK viticulture—combining weather and climate records with UK producers' perspectives" spells out the trade-offs for English wines and for many other regions.[8] The study found a "nonlinear" warming trend in the main winegrowing regions over the last several decades. Higher growing-season temperatures have encouraged growers to plant more Chardonnay and Pinot Noir, highly desirable grapes for sparkling wine, but they are also varieties that are sensitive to weather anomalies such as late frosts or unseasonable rainstorms. May frosts and June rainstorms can undo the benefits of a warm April. In short, increases in weather variability can offset the benefits of warming for UK grape producers. The fact that some have shifted away from cooler-climate grape varieties increases the industry's vulnerability to negative weather events.

Will increased weather volatility act to limit the migration from warmer to cooler wine regions in the U.K., Tasmania, and elsewhere around the globe? Hard to know, if only because things seem to be changing so quickly. My wine travels have taken me to many places where the weather seemed wrong. I went to speak to a winegrower group in Ontario, Canada, in March 2015, for example, only to find vines still covered in snow, which was a good thing since it insulated them from the unseasonably late bitter cold. The view from my hotel window was the frozen Niagara River. Now that's cold. A trip back from Virginia wine country to Seattle featured the fastest east-to-west transcontinental flight of my life. The jet stream, which usually creates a strong headwind, was nowhere to be found having been diverted by unusual pressure patterns. We pulled into the SeaTac gate more than an hour ahead of schedule. California winegrowers have lived through several years of record drought relieved by just the opposite—record rains. Normal weather? I have no idea what that means anymore.

Meanwhile, back in Tasmania, we are reminded that climate change is a complicated phenomenon. A February 2016 article in *The Economist* proclaims, "Tasmania Charts a New Course: Water into Wine."[9] Tasmania's weather may or may not be getting more volatile, but this article reminds us that changes are happening almost everywhere. Tasmania has just 1 percent of Australia's landmass and 2 percent of its population, but it gratefully receives 13 percent of its rainfall (although it doesn't all fall in the most convenient or useful places). So long as mainland Australia (Tazzies call it "the big island") remains the driest continent on earth, with droughts increasingly frequent, cooler, wetter Tasmania will exert a magnetic pull. Because in today's warming world, it really is hot to be cool.

⌇

The Wines

Tolpuddle Pinot Noir, Coal River, Tasmania, Australia

Domaine A Cabernet Sauvignon, Coal River, Tasmania, Australia

Nyetimber Classic Cuvée, Sussex, England

⌇

Chapter 12

Southern Cross

"Southern Cross" is the title of a tune that became popular with the release of the 1982 Crosby, Stills & Nash album *Daylight Again.*[1] The song seems at first to be about a sailor's voyage in the South Pacific, where he sees the Southern Cross, that hemisphere's distinctive star-scape. But as you listen to it and its beautiful harmonies, it becomes apparent that the song is really the story of love, life, loss, and what endures.

If chapters of this book had theme songs, which I guess they don't, this chapter's would be "Southern Cross" and not just because we are going to be sailing to New Zealand and then on to South America in the company of those famous bright stars. Each stop will teach us something about loss and redemption and maybe also about what endures. Are you up for our wine-driven, star-guided journey?

ROMEO IN NEW ZEALAND

The year is 1895 and we are sailing from Australia to New Zealand in the company of a Dalmatian wine expert with the extravagant name Romeo Alessandro Bragato, one of the great pioneers of New Zealand wine. Trained at the famous Italian wine school in Conegliano, not far from Venice, Bragato was hired in 1889 to help develop a wine industry in Australia's Victoria region. So useful were his efforts that in 1895 New Zealand Prime Minister Richard

Seddon requested that the Victoria government lend him Bragato so that he could assess the potential for a Kiwi wine industry.

Bragato surveyed the islands from north to south and he found lots of winegrowing potential. This will come as no surprise when you realize that the twin islands that together form New Zealand stretch pretty much from the coolest conventional wine climate at the southernmost end to the warmest typical wine zone up north closest to the equator. There are all types of natural conditions between south and north, seemingly something and somewhere for every wine. Bragato's analysis, published as *Prospects for Viticulture in New Zealand*, pointed the way forward for Kiwi wine. Bragato didn't bring wine grapes to New Zealand (by most accounts the first grapevines were planted by the Reverend Samuel Marsden at Kerikeri on the Bay of Islands on the North Island in 1816), but he did bring professional expertise and a vision of a wine industry future.[2]

Bragato returned to New Zealand several times, especially monitoring the incidence of phylloxera and promoting the use of phylloxera-resistant rootstock, before accepting a post in 1902 as New Zealand Department of Agriculture chief viticulturalist. His tenure was significant in terms of science and industry—he published the authoritative *Viticulture in New Zealand*—but not especially long-lived. A strong temperance movement swept through the islands and the Department of Agriculture shut down its wine program. Disgusted, Bragato and his family sulked away to British Columbia, Canada, in 1909. He died there in 1913 at the age of fifty-five years.

It is hard not to think of Romeo Bragato now because the vibrant wine industry that he imagined has come to pass, perhaps exceeding even his grandest dreams. New Zealand today is nearly as well known for its wine as for its hobbits (the *Lord of the Rings* films were made here). You can find cool-climate Pinot Noir in Central Otago, pungent Sauvignon Blanc in Marlborough, and heat-loving red wines in Hawkes Bay, to name just three of the many regions. Although New Zealand's total wine production is tiny (it is the seventeenth largest wine-producing nation in the world, sandwiched between Hungary and Austria in the league table) its distribution is wide. And it sells for a premium price. Indeed, New Zealand's average export price typically tops the global list for still table wines. Amazing, especially since a white wine, Sauvignon Blanc, leads the way and red wines often command higher status and prices.

Wine in New Zealand went through a number of cycles over the decades since Romeo Bragato bolted to Canada. Waves of immigrants brought wine with them when they fled pre–World War I Central Europe seeking peace and prosperity, for example. But war, depression, and other problems always seemed to keep the industry from thriving. Then, in the 1970s, the government adopted a closed economy economic development strategy designed to stimulate domestic growth by keeping foreign products and investment out. It was a disaster, at least for the wine industry. Minus foreign competition, New Zealand wine became a race to the bottom, with low-quality products meant to satisfy a least-common-denominator market. The market collapsed and a government-financed "grubbing-up" program was implemented to literally tear the uneconomic vines from the land. New Zealand wine hit rock bottom.

Having failed to grow industry with protectionist hothouse tactics, the government reversed course generally, and with respect to wine in particular. Barriers to foreign products and investment fell away. Cheap foreign wines flooded in, taking the market that Kiwi wines previously held as a monopoly. The only way to survive in wine was to move upmarket and focus on export. That this movement was successful is tribute both to Romeo Bragato's vision for New Zealand and also to the tenacity and determination of the winemakers and entrepreneurs who rose to the challenge of the brave new wine world.

Two wines go into our eighty-bottle case to represent New Zealand. The first is a Pinot Noir from Quartz Reef in Central Otago. Romeo Bragato visited this cool region at the southern part of the southern island and declared it ideal for wine. Especially, he noted, the Pinot Noir with which it is now identified.

Quartz Reef is a single-vineyard wine made by a small firm established in the 1990s by an Austrian winemaker who came south when the wine market here opened up. The Quartz Reef Pinot and sparkling wines get strong reviews, with the Pinot Gris often singled out for special praise. Quartz Reef represents the successful craft wine industry that Romeo Bragato might have imagined.

Brancott Estate, the second of the New Zealand wines I have selected, goes beyond whatever Bragato might have dreamed. It is named after the original Brancott Estate, which was the first Sauvignon Blanc vineyard in the Marlborough region at the top of the South Island. Marlborough might have been the last place that Bragato would have expected to see wine grapes. It is notably absent from his survey of the islands' most promising regions. And indeed wine grapes were not important in Marlborough until the tariff and investment barriers came falling down and the internationalization of New Zealand wine gathered force.

Fortified with funding from Canada's Seagram's company, Ivan Yukich and his son Frankie planted the Brancott Estate vineyard and, with the help of a host of others, soon Marlborough Sauvignon Blanc was a success in the British market and then beyond. Although there is much more to New Zealand than Pinot Noir and Sauvignon Blanc, their strong reputations define Kiwi wine on global markets today.

The Yukich family's Montana Winery was eventually purchased by the French multinational drinks company Pernod Ricard, which now sells the wines worldwide. The Montana brand was changed to Brancott Estate for the U.S. market (to avoid confusion that the wines might come from the state of Montana!) and eventually the whole company was rebranded Brancott Estate in honor of the famous vineyard. Much of the New Zealand wine industry is now in foreign multinational hands. Cloudy Bay, for example, is part of the French LVMH luxury goods group and Kim Crawford belongs to Constellation, the large U.S. wine and beer producer. If Romeo Bragato were alive today he might shake his head. I knew the wines would be good. But I didn't see that coming!

CHILE AND WHAT ENDURES

It's a long way from New Zealand to Chile, just over 5,600 miles as the crow flies, much farther than the journey from Tasmania to Marlborough. Chile and New Zealand are very far apart both in distance and in winemaking scale. Chile is the world's sixth largest wine producer by volume after the Big Three (Italy, France, and Spain), the United States, and Argentina.[3] Chile's total yearly production is more than five times the amount of wine made in New Zealand.

But the two countries have some things in common. Both are thin strips of land arrayed south to north, spanning the conventional wine latitudes. And both are isolated. New Zealand is isolated because the islands are a long way from anywhere else. Chile is functionally an island, isolated by the Pacific

Ocean to the west and the steep Andes mountains to the east. This isolation is both a challenge to the Chilean wine industry (as it is to the Kiwis) and was an unexpected blessing during the era when phylloxera was sweeping the wine world.

Wine was brought to Chile by Spanish missionaries and priests much earlier (1554) than English and French missionaries arrived with grapevines in New Zealand. A local wine industry developed in Chile beyond religious use and was successful enough to become a problem by the seventeenth century. Spanish wine producers saw a profitable export market in the New World colonies undermined by local production and convinced the king to ban new plantings in Mexico, Chile, and elsewhere to encourage sales of wines from Spain.

The modern Chilean wine industry took root after independence from Spain and by the 1850s a large selection of pre-phylloxera French grape varieties had been planted, which supplemented the grapes that the missionaries brought three centuries before. The timing was critical here because just a few years later phylloxera spread around the world (Bragato found it near Auckland during his New Zealand survey). But it has not yet invaded Chilean vineyards, even after all these years, and so you find here a rare thing: *Vitis vinifera* vines growing on their own rootstocks.

Chilean wines found ready markets in Europe and elsewhere during the dark days when phylloxera limited production in other regions and they were well received, setting an early pattern for Chile as an export-oriented wine industry. The industry went through many ups and downs, suffering in particular during the authoritarian Pinochet regime when Chile's reputation around the world sank to a deep low. This changed with the restoration of democracy and, as in New Zealand, the implementation of free market policies that encouraged inward investment and outward export growth.[4]

Chilean wine today is dominated by four large firms, the biggest of which was founded by Don Melchor Concha y Toro in 1883 (at the height of the phylloxera epidemic in Europe). Viña Concha y Toro is today Latin America's largest wine producer and one of the largest vineyard owners in the world. In 2014 and again in 2015 Concha y Toro was named the "World's Most Powerful Wine Brand."[5] Most consumers are probably familiar with the Casillero del Diablo brand, but Concha y Toro produces an incredible range of wines from the traditional Frontera brand Pais (the Mission grape) on up to top-of-the-line icon Don Melchor Cabernet Sauvignon.

Many wine consumers who drink from the Devil's Cellar (Casillero del Diablo) are probably unaware of Concha y Toro's focus on sustainability, including organic and even biodynamic production. This was the idea behind the launch of the Cono Sur winery in 1993 and this project has grown tremendously over the years. The value-priced "bicycle label" wines are widely distributed and the lineup extends to a limited-production "20 Barrels" line and Ocio, an iconic Pinot Noir. Concha y Toro continues to grow, with investments in Argentina, partnerships with the Rothschilds of France and, in 2011, the purchase of Fetzer and Bonterra, U.S. wineries known for their sustainable practices.

Chile adds an interesting theme to our Southern Cross tune because it takes the New Zealand saga of love, loss, and renewal and adds a complicated story of endurance. Many things have endured in Chilean wine, especially the pre-phylloxera vines, which are today a significant genetic resource. The fact that the Carmenère grape variety endured here is doubly important since that Bordeaux grape was not widely replanted in post-phylloxera France because of low yields. And of course the culture of wine endured political turmoil and dictatorship only to emerge with vigor in the democratic era.

But not everything that has endured has been a gift. Although wine drinkers around the world are happy that Chilean wines remain both good and good value, I know many producers there feel that their best wines are ignored or perhaps just underappreciated because consumers still think of Chilean wines as great wine values, not as great wines. The wines seem to get better every year, but stereotypes are slow to change. Chile's wine reputation is a work in progress.

Our visit to Chile is much too brief, but we need to find an airplane to fly over the Andes. It is not too far to drive from Santiago to Mendoza, but the truck-filled mountain roads intimidate me. Argentina adds the final verse to our Southern Cross recording.

BOOM AND BUST

Malbec is the star in Argentina—the most-planted red grape and the signature wine variety. It might not be the country's best wine—I know friends who swear they prefer the Cabernet Sauvignon or other varieties, and there have been periods when Malbec vines were pulled up in favor of other grapes—but when I first started studying Argentina ten years ago, the big story was Malbec's amazing rise.[6] For a time Argentina was second only to New Zealand in market growth in the U.S. for example. Ten years later Argentina is still a success story, but not the boomtown phenomenon it once was. Whatever happened to Argentina's wine boom, and can that country's wine industry recover the momentum it has lost?

These questions about Argentina's wine industry echo concerns that have been expressed over the years about the country itself. Go back in time a little over one hundred years and you will find the country booming on the basis of its natural resource exports. Incredibly, Argentines had the highest average per capita wealth in the world according to one study and it was common to say that someone was "rich as an Argentine." Buenos Aires was the "Paris of the South" and we saw at least one building that was actually Parisian—it had been taken apart stone by stone in Paris and reassembled here. But the boom turned to bust, a recurring cycle, and Argentina has been unable to achieve its obvious potential.

The recent wine boom had many causes. Perhaps the most important was the Argentine peso crisis of the early 2000s. The collapse of the peso and the opening of the economy to foreign investment was a painful transition for the people of Argentina, but it restored international competitiveness and encouraged foreign investment, both critical to the wine industry's rise.

As in many European countries, wine consumption in Argentina is in steep long-term decline and the peso crisis made things worse for the domestic market, where inexpensive jug wines dominate. As detailed in Laura Catena's book *Vino Argentino* and Ian Mount's *The Vineyard at the End of the World*, Argentine producers found themselves with no choice but to focus on export markets for growth, and that meant major investments to improve quality. The U.S. market was the prime target, a different strategy from Chile, which developed more diversified export opportunities.[7]

The U.S.-led export push was effective for several reasons. First the wines presented good value and rapidly improving quality. The U.S. wine market was growing and consumers were turning away from Merlot and later Syrah/Shiraz, opening the door for easy-to-drink and -understand Malbec. Some of the most important brands established effective distribution partnerships, which enabled them to lead Argentina into the market and firmly establish the category. Catena partnered with Gallo, for example, to make Alamos the market leader. No wonder Argentina's wine exports boomed year after year. The only questions, it seemed at the time, were whether demand would continue to rise and, if it did, could Argentina produce enough Malbec to satisfy thirsty buyers?

And then? Well, the boom didn't turn to bust as many feared, but Argentina's export growth skidded to a stop. It seems to me that the most severe constraint on Argentina exports in recent years has been supply, not demand. The economic policies of the government of President Cristina Fernández de Kirchner raised inflation rates, which pushed up wage rates, which increased the cost of producing wine. At the same time, the exchange rate was frozen at an artificially high rate, which squeezed margins. Capital controls added to the problem by making it difficult for Argentina to import technology and winemaking supplies from abroad. The inflation/exchange rate squeeze was particularly hard on the value wine exports that were the initial key to Argentina's success. It was nearly impossible to profit from exports of Argentine Malbec with a retail price below about ten dollars, so many of these wines have simply disappeared from the market (a few brave firms absorbed short-term losses to maintain their market positions for the future).

The country changed directions in December 2015 when Mauricio Macri became president of Argentina, promising an end to the policies that crippled the economy, especially export industries like wine. But some of my friends in Argentina tell me that they are not expecting a miracle. They just want Argentina to be "like a normal country," as they put it, in terms of its politics and economics and perhaps that's what they will get. If "normalization" works, will Argentina's wine export boom return? Perhaps, but times have changed and just adjusting the macroeconomic levers won't turn back the clock entirely. Argentina will come back, that's for sure, although it will take a while for the foreign exchange and other factors to be fully felt.

The best that Argentina should hope for—and it is actually a good thing—is to be like a "normal country" when it comes to the U.S. wine market. By this I mean that its exports are driven by the normal factors and not subject to booms or crises. Being a normal country means resisting the temptation to define Argentina exclusively as Malbec-ville. I know the temptation to adopt a particular grape as a region's "signature variety" is strong, but I don't see it as the best path for the industry. Argentina has Malbec, and that's a good thing. But before the growth slowed, smart Argentinean producers were already trying to add dimensions to their market space. *Terroir* is an obvious dimension that is even more important in signaling quality and authenticity than it was a few years ago. I think many consumers now look for region—Uco Valley? Salta?—and especially elevation (Malbec seems to develop differently at different heights in Argentina) as quality indicators.

Another way to add dimensions is to exploit grape varieties beyond Malbec. There are so many wines that do well in Argentina besides Malbec and Torrontes, the two "designated" signature grapes. I love Mendel's Sémillon (the ungrafted vines are seventy-five years old), for example, and we recently surprised a Syrah-loving friend at a local Argentine restaurant by ordering a higher-elevation Syrah from the Uco Valley. He loved it, but would never have thought of ordering an Argentine Syrah. This is an age of discovery for wine and Argentina has much to discover, both within the Malbec *terroirs* and beyond Malbec. That's the sort of strategy that "normal countries" are embracing in the U.S. wine market today.

Argentina has little experience as a normal country, making its way without crisis or drama. The success of Macri's economic policies is not a sure thing since they depend on short-term sacrifice for long-term gains in an uncertain and even unstable global economic environment. It won't be easy to become normal, but it is an important step.

Sometimes, as Argentina's national soccer team has demonstrated, great players and great ideas can come to a disappointing end. I am optimistic, however, and hopeful that the wine sector will regain momentum—that it will endure—while avoiding the boom-bust cycles of the past. To honor this thought I add three more wines to our growing list, the Nicolás Catena Zapata Cabernet Sauvignon–Malbec, Mendel Wines' Old Vine Sémillon and Colomé Auténtico Malbec, from vines grown at 7,700 feet up north in Salta. Catena and his colleagues pushed for higher quality, the team at Mendel made sure the old vines would endure even as they pushed ahead in quality. The Colomé Auténico Malbec is intentionally made in an old style—no oak, lots of soak time—that pays tribute to the past while simultaneously opening up new market opportunities.

I hope someday to visit Salta—it is on my bucket list—and to toast the life, loss, and love that is part of the story of wine (and the answer to that "why wine?" question) and the things that endure. Sitting there high in the Andes I imagine the stars of the Southern Cross will be especially bright.

〜

The Wines

Quartz Reef Pinot Noir, Central Otago, New Zealand

Brancott Estate Sauvignon Blanc, Marlborough, New Zealand

Concha y Toro Casillero del Diablo Carmenère, Chile

Nicolás Catena Zapata Cabernet Sauvignon–Malbec, Mendoza, Argentina

Mendel Wines Sémillon, Mendoza, Argentina

Colomé Auténtico Malbec, Salta, Argentina

〜

Part IV
SOUR GRAPES?

Chapter 13

Napa Valley Wine Train

It was seven o'clock in the morning when Phileas Fogg, Passepartout, and Aouda disembarked from their steamship, setting foot on a floating quay that led to a pier that connected to the San Francisco shore. They hurried to get breakfast and have their passports stamped at the British embassy, but they didn't waste any time. They had a train to catch at six o'clock that evening. Their Central Pacific train would take them from the Oakland station to Ogden, Utah, where they would transfer to a Union Pacific train for the trip to Omaha, Nebraska, where they would choose the fastest of five possible lines to New York and another steamship voyage, this time home to London.

Time was of the essence so the promised efficiency of the American train system was just the ticket. If all went according to plan (which—spoiler alert!—it did not) the long journey could be accomplished in just seven days. Amazing! But the West was still wild in 1872 and Passepartout thought it wise to purchase "some dozens of Enfield rifles and Colt's revolvers" just in case some kind of trouble found them. Unnecessary, Fogg thought, but do what you think best.

RIDING THE WINE RAILS

We are also in San Francisco to catch a train, but our journey is much shorter (a few hours max), our direction different (north not east), and the weapon of choice will be a corkscrew, not a gun or even a knife (although a knife might come in handy in case we need to cut up some salami or cheese to munch on). We are taking the wine train to the Napa Valley to try to understand the California wine scene.

The first winery in Napa Valley, Charles Krug, was founded in 1861 and train service began three years later.[1] A ferry from San Francisco dropped passengers in Vallejo, where they continued north by rail to the resort town of Calistoga. Tourism was a big part of the line's purpose right from the start. Passenger trains ran until 1929 and freight trains continued to operate until 1985, when normal commercial operations more or less stopped.

Enter entrepreneur Vincent DeDomenico, who made a splash as president of the Golden Grain company, famous in these parts for a rice and vermicelli pilaf called Rice-a-Roni ("the San Francisco treat" according to an advertising jingle). Some of the money DeDomenico received from selling Golden Grain and Ghirardelli Chocolate to the Quaker Oats company in 1986 financed the creation of the Napa Valley Railroad, which acquired use of the rails and announced plans for a Wine Train to take tourists from San Francisco to Napa Valley once again. But this time they would visit the famous wineries there, not take the waters in Calistoga.

You might expect that Napa Valley residents would welcome this new enterprise, with its nod to valley history, quaint old-fashioned locomotive, Pullman passenger cars, and tourism dollar potential. But you would be wrong. Instead, it seems, they took up arms against the plan (figurative arms—put down that Enfield). More noise, more tourists, more congestion. Not in our backyard. But operations were approved and the controversial wine train service began. At this writing the train brings more than a hundred thousand passengers to the valley each year.

The DeDomenico family sold the Wine Train operation to a Seattle-based hospitality group in 2015, which expanded service to include a six-hour tour called Quattro Vini, with winery stops at Robert Mondavi, Charles Krug, Merryvale, and V. Sattui, and a three-course tasting meal en route. Tickets start at $249 per person. A variety of other options focus on particular wineries (Raymond or Grgich Hills, for example) or the vintage train experience itself. Tickets for the Raymond tour, which includes lunch, tour, and tasting, start at $189. A monthly excursion called Romance on the Rails doesn't seem to stop anywhere, but features the romantic ride, passing scenery, and a gourmet meal. Tickets start at $234.[2]

WINE TOURING NAPA-STYLE

What brings tourists to the Napa Valley today? Well trains and cars and sometimes even hot-air balloons bring them in the literal sense, but what draws them here is something more. Once upon a time people visited wineries to buy wine to take home—shopping more than touring. And this is still the case in many parts of the wine world today. But the people who come to Napa are looking for more. They want an experience (and they usually get it).

I give Robert Mondavi some of the credit for this transformation. I have called Mondavi "the Julia Child of wine." Julia Child used the mass media of her time to teach us that food was an experience, not just something you made and ate. She both entertained and intrigued us and made us all want to tap into a cosmopolitan culinary lifestyle. Mondavi realized that wine needed to be more than an alcoholic beverage if it was to blossom in post-Prohibition America. Wine needed to be linked to romance, culture, history, music, food, and luxury lifestyle, so he built a winery that looked like a California hacienda more than a factory and filled the calendar with concerts, dinners, tours, and tastings. The Robert Mondavi winery was more than a winery, it was (and is) a destination, and the guests who visit leave as brand ambassadors for Mondavi and Napa, too. I've never met anyone who had a bad visit to Mondavi. Robert Mondavi and his team were not alone is this vision, but they certainly led the way.

The Mondavi family no longer controls the Robert Mondavi Winery (it is now part of the Constellation Brands portfolio), but you can get a sense of how the vision has evolved by visiting the Mondavi hacienda. The distinctive architecture is still there, of course, as is the famous To Kalon vineyard and the warm welcome that guests receive. A regular calendar of concerts and art displays is maintained as per the Mondavi philosophy. Walk-in visitors can just taste wines (fees range from $5 to $30 per person, depending on the wines you choose), or you can tour the facility in small groups. A thirty-minute tour with tasting of two wines is $20 and a ninety-minute tour in Mandarin is available for $35, but other options range up to a ninety-minute twilight walking tour (the vineyard is beautiful in the fading light) with special wine tasting and savory snacks for $55.

You can also schedule an opportunity to learn to pair the Mondavi wines with chocolate or cheese ($45 for sixty to ninety minutes) or spend an hour tasting and snacking in the To Kalon barrel room for $55. The "Harvest of Joy" tour and lunch takes two and a half hours and costs $115. There's a four-hour "Garden to Table" dinner for $150 per person or, for that special occasion, the "Five Decade" tasting menu dinner with wines from each decade of the winery's history. It is yours by special arrangement for $350 per guest. Selfies in front of the winery are priceless and very popular and they remain free of charge to all.

The Robert Mondavi Winery really is a destination and it handles a large number of visitors each day with well-organized grace and apparent ease. The high volume permits a degree of specialization that isn't possible for every winery. But the state of the art here focuses on designing wine tourist experiences that go well beyond the traditional tasting bar protocols infamously parodied in the "dump bucket" scene of the 2004 film *Sideways*. Wineries want visitors to slow down, reset, focus, and soak up the story of the place. Tasting is part of that but not always the most important part since tastes differ so much and most people are not accustomed to sampling through several different wines at a single sitting. Wine is good, but wine and a story can be memorable.

Thus the modern Napa winery carefully crafts the visitor experience from first impression to final gift-shop goodbye. Some wineries employ a concierge at the cellar door to engage guests in casual conversation and, after learning a bit about them, direct them to just the right experience for their interest level, time schedule, and budget. All of this is expensive, which accounts for some of the relatively high fees charged for these activities, but price is also used as an allocation tool so that scarce resources go to those with greater interest or at least higher credit card limits. Most wineries also have special "behind the scenes" events, including vineyard harvest days, for their best customers and winery club members as well as visiting retailers, distributors, or sommeliers.

One winery, V. Sattui (which is part of the Wine Train tour), is known in the valley for selling all of its wine directly to visitors. The family's latest enterprise is a pure wine tourism play. Castello di Amorosa is an "authentically built thirteenth-century Tuscan castle." It is quite a spectacular achievement, although surely also a bit of a folly. It's not really clear that Napa Valley needs a thirteenth-century Tuscan castle or a castle of any kind. Still it is far from the only extravagant winery destination in the area and a reminder that many locals might well have shaken their heads in disbelief when Mondavi's hacienda broke ground. A guided tour and tasting at the castle will cost you forty or fifty dollars, depending upon the wines, with the chance to upgrade with cheese or chocolate pairings and more. Castello di Amorosa gets high ratings on Yelp (where its prices are ranked "moderate" for Napa Valley by users) and is the number one (of sixty-five) things to do in Calistoga on TripAdvisor.

So what do you get when you have over four hundred wineries in a fairly compact region and most of them are involved to a greater or lesser extent in the touring, tasting, and hospitality business? The local tourist authority, Visit Napa Valley, commissioned a study of the economic impact of wine tourism in 2014 and here's what they found.[3]

About 3.3 million visitors came to Napa Valley in 2014, according to estimates, spending a total of 5.4 million visit-days there. This puts Napa Valley a long way behind Disneyland in Anaheim, California, which is the state's largest tourist draw with 16.7 million visitors in 2014. But Napa is not so far behind Yosemite National Park, which had about 4 million visitors that year. This translates into over fifteen thousand Napa visitors on an average day, which is just a bit scary when you consider that most of them have been drinking or at least tasting alcoholic beverages. Makes you thankful that the traffic on Highway 29 sometimes slows to a low-impact crawl!

About two-thirds of Napa's wine tourists were day-trippers in 2014—in and out in the same day like the wine train's passengers. More than 28 percent stayed in hotels, motels, or resorts in the valley, however, generating jobs and income in the lodging sector. Altogether the tourists spent about $1.63 billion here, including $375 million for food and restaurants. The study estimates that more than eleven thousand jobs were thus supported with a total payroll of $332 million. Clearly wine tourism is big business, both for the wineries like Robert Mondavi and for the whole region. Napa Valley just might be the most successful place in the world in terms of its wine tourist experience. A wine lover's paradise. What could go wrong?

TROUBLE IN PARADISE

Wineries and wine tourism have made Napa Valley the famous place that it is today. But how many wineries (and tourists) are enough? When I travel to other parts of the wine world, the people I meet cannot imagine ever asking a question like this. Too many? Too much? You've got to be kidding me. Bring on the enthusiasts and their dollars, euros, yen, and pesos. The more the merrier. I suppose that the Napa Valley was like that once, but as the people who created the Napa Valley Wine Train learned twenty-five years ago, that time has passed. Now each and every proposal to build a new winery, expand an existing one, give wineries permits to welcome more guests (yes, guest numbers are regulated in Napa Valley), or host more events is questioned, scrutinized, debated, and sometimes actively opposed.

One way I follow this debate is by reading the insightful columns that Paul Franson writes for the *Napa Valley Register*. His reports on committee meetings and regulatory approval hearings give a visceral sense of the tension between and among Napa's many identities and interests, including an activist group called Napa Vision 2050.[4] Tourism and hospitality (and the incomes they generate) are weighed against residential lifestyle and agricultural identity, for example, and economic development versus health and environment concerns. It is a complicated situation with strong feelings on all sides. Asked to list the top ten local wine stories of 2015, Franson put the record drought first, the unusually small crop second, and the winery and tourism controversy third. "Public outcry led to an intense discussion of wineries, their production, and visitors and events," he wrote. ". . . [B]ut nothing is resolved yet. Few expect huge changes."[5] And so the tempers will continue to smolder and tensions slowly build.

I don't want to add any fuel to the debate (after some years I have finally come to terms with the snail pace of traffic on the tourist-clogged Napa roads), but I see one more problem with Napa Valley's great success. So many people come to the valley for the day and see the vineyards and wineries and taste the wines that they come away with what might be a distorted sense of reality. They start to think that Napa is California and California is the whole wine world. They lose track of the truth, which is that California is a big place where the wine industry has developed in different ways, many of which are different from the Napa pattern and the controversies are quite different, too.

One antidote to the Napa syndrome, for example, is to visit the Ramona Valley wine region, which is located in the rocky foothills about an hour's drive from San Diego. This is a very scenic region where visitors come to play tennis and ride horses. The Mexican food here is great, as you might expect, being so close to the border, and the specialty at local restaurants is chicken-fried steak! Turkey production was once a big deal here, but now grapes and wine are making news. Some of the wines we tasted were great, so there is potential, but no one we met thinks there are too many vineyards, wineries, or tourists. Just the opposite—bring them on! For most wine regions of the world, the reality may be closer to Ramona than Napa on these issues.

THE GLASSES OF THE MASSES: TWO-BUCK CHUCK

If you weigh California wine by dollar value per bottle or ton of wine grapes, then Napa Valley comes out on top every time. But if you are interested in wines of the people, wines that sell in large volumes and fill the glasses of the masses, then you have to look elsewhere and, when you get there, you won't find too many wine tourists around. The wineries are large and have an industrial feel when compared with Napa haciendas or boutique châteaux. And the vineyards, many of them in the hot San Joaquin Valley, have much more of an authentic agricultural feel, too. Wine tourists? No, the people who come here are on a business mission.

But that doesn't mean that a visitor wouldn't have an interesting wine experience. Sue and I thoroughly enjoyed ourselves when we accepted an invitation from Fred Franzia, head of Bronco Wines and Mr. "Two-Buck Chuck," to visit the production facility in Ceres, California. If a wine train runs through Ceres, I'll bet it hauls wine, not tourists.

Bronco Wine Company is a major force in the U.S. wine industry. According to *Wine Business Monthly* report, Bronco's 20 million annual case volume makes it the fourth largest U.S. wine company after Gallo, The Wine Group, and Constellation Brands. Although Charles Shaw (aka Two-Buck Chuck) is the best known Bronco label, the company has more than fifty brands. One of the products that Bronco does not make is Franzia, the popular box wine, which belongs to The Wine Group. Fred Franzia doesn't make Franzia? It's a long story that I will tell another time.

Bronco's history began in 1973, when Fred Franzia and his brother Joseph met with their cousin John and pledged to go all in to build a new wine company. Fortified with a tiny bank loan, their knowledge of the business side (Fred and Joseph) and of winemaking (John), plus a major measure of determination, they set out on the twisting road that has brought them to their current position. Their accomplishment is quite breathtaking when you think about it. Bronco today boasts impressive winemaking facilities, a packaging and distribution center in Napa, and about forty thousand acres of vineyards. No, I didn't make a mistake, the number is forty thousand, making Bronco one of the largest vineyard owners in the world.

One of Bronco's greatest achievements is the success of the Charles Shaw wines sold at Trader Joe's stores. Despite its limited distribution, this wine became a phenomenon and, in 2016, Fred Franzia announced the sale of the one billionth bottle of the wine, which caused Paul Franson to do the math (1,000,000,000 × $2) and label him Two-Billion-Buck Chuck.[6] The wines don't sell for two dollars anymore, but at $2.49 or $2.99 or a little more, they remain spectacular values. There was quite a scene a few years ago when the 2005 Charles Shaw wine won the prize for "Best Chardonnay" in a blind taste test at the prestigious California State Fair Competition. Was the wine a fake, some people questioned incredulously? Winemaking veteran Richard Peterson bought some to find out and concluded that it was the inexpensive wine's precise balance that explained the award. In a roomful of cult wines that push all the extreme buttons, he proposed, a really well-balanced wine can stand out, as it apparently did here.[7]

These clean, balanced, and affordable wines played an important role in the democratization of wine in the United States. Many previously intimidated consumers were drawn into the wine market by Two-Buck Chuck and the other wines it inspired or provoked. The quality of these inexpensive wines forced other winemakers to raise their game and give better value, which in turn gave consumers more confidence and expanded the wine market's reach. If you think about the U.S. wine world before 1973, well, it really is a miracle that we have come so far. The Franzias played an important role in that transformation.

Fred invited us to come down to see what a large-scale grape harvest looks like. Fred's son Joey took us to see the night harvest at a four-thousand-acre vineyard ranch near Lodi—quite an experience to see the big machines at work under the stars. We also visited the Napa bottling and distribution center and the main winery in Ceres, where we had lunch with Fred, Joseph, and John Franzia. Then John took us through the working winery (he designed it and supervised its construction), which was receiving grapes picked the night before (more than three hundred big truckloads a day at that time).

The scale of the Ceres operation got our attention, of course. We saw some tanks that held 350,000 gallons of wine each. Big as they are, they were dwarfed by other tanks that held even more. Amazing. Once we got used to the scale of the Bronco winery we began to appreciate the tremendous attention to detail, which was apparent in all of the other Bronco operations we visited. So many moving parts coordinated so efficiently. Very impressive. We enjoyed the opportunity to sit and chat with Fred in his modest trailer office and to learn his vision of the future. Bronco is highly focused on organic production and environmental sustainability, for example, as it was in the process of converting ten thousand acres to organic vineyards at that time.

Fred told us many stories and this is my favorite. He was making a call at a Trader Joe's store—he still handles that account himself—and struck up a conversation with a young man who was stocking a Charles Shaw display. Fred asked how the wine was selling and what customers were saying and so on, and the clerk asked who he was and why he wanted to know. Well, Fred replied, I'm one of the people who help make this wine—I work at the winery.

Wow, the clerk exclaimed. You're Charles Shaw? *You're Charlie Shaw!* No, no, my name's not Shaw, Fred tried to explain, but it was too late and a minute later the store PA system announced that Charles Shaw was visiting the wine aisle. Amazed customers surged to the Two-Buck Chuck display to thank their hero and Fred spent the rest of his visit happily autographing wine bottles. A rock-star moment!

The night harvest in Lodi and tour of the Ceres facility with its big tanks and tiny offices is not rated on Yelp or TripAdvisor as far as I can see. No tasting was offered and no tasting fee charged. No one tried to upsell us to the reserve wines or pair chocolate or cheese, although Fred did take us to lunch as a little roadside place where I had the best tri-tip beef sandwich of my life.

WHAT IS CALIFORNIA WINE?

So what is California wine all about? Is it the Disneyland of Napa, when it is flooded with tourists as it can be during the famous Auction Napa Valley, which raises millions for charity? Is it the quiet, rustic charm of Ramona Valley? Or is it the large-scale agriculture and production winemaking we saw at Bronco? The answer, as you have already guessed, is that it is all of these things and more. Guests on the Napa Valley Wine Train experience a particular idea of California wine, but one that could never fill the glasses of the masses.

So what wines should we select? There are more than four thousand wineries in California, so it is impossible to do more than scratch the surface. We begin with Two-Buck Chuck, since that is a wine that helped create the miracle of America's status among world wine consumer nations: Number one in total wine purchases (at least until the Chinese catch up). And then of course a wine from Robert Mondavi—I will choose the To Kalon Fumé Blanc.

I wrote the first draft of this chapter on May 24, which is the anniversary of the 1976 "Judgment of Paris" tasting where California wines proved their quality in a blind tasting with great French wines. Allow me to include a Stag's Leap Wine Cellars Cabernet Sauvignon in our traveling case to honor the wine that topped the red wine table on that historic day.[8]

⌢

The Wines
Charles Shaw Chardonnay, California
Robert Mondavi To Kalon Fumé Blanc, Napa Valley, California
Stag's Leap Wine Cellars Cabernet Sauvignon, Napa Valley, California

⌢

Chapter 14

A Riesling Rendezvous

There are two main routes north from Napa Valley. Highway 101 is the more attractive drive, offering tall redwood forests, dramatic Crater Lake, and beautiful Oregon beaches, but it can be slow as scenic highways often are. Interstate 5 lacks romance, but it is pretty efficient. Either way, you want to end up near the heart of Willamette Valley wine country at McMinnville, Oregon, where the International Pinot Noir Celebration takes place each July on the grounds of Linfield College.

The wine world is full of festivals, conferences, and symposia of many sorts. Some are created for consumers pure and simple, with dozens of wine-makers pouring hundreds of their wines to guests who have paid something for the right to a bottomless wineglass and lots of tasty snacks. Other meetings are there for trade and industry. I often speak, for example, at the Unified Wine & Grape Symposium in Sacramento, California. More than fourteen thousand wine industry people purchase tickets for three days of seminars (some of which are offered in both English and Spanish) and to gain access to the huge trade show floor. It is the largest wine industry gathering in the Western Hemisphere and I am pretty sure that it is all business. Nobody attends the Unified Symposium solely to sniff, swirl, and snack.

The IPNC as it is called is a hybrid of these two models. Great food and wine (almost all Pinot Noir as you would expect from the name, in both still and sparkling forms), with gala dinners and grand tastings. The Saturday night barbecued salmon dinner on the lawn under the towering oak trees with the stars and moon above is quite an experience, especially with a winemaker host at each table. No wonder Pinot-loving enthusiasts come back year after year. But there is a lot of business and networking that takes place here behind the scenes. Good fun and good business, too.

The nice thing about events like the Pinot festival is that you don't have to travel around the world to taste the world's wines and meet the world's wine people. They come to you. The 2016 IPNC featured U.S. wineries from Oregon, California, Washington, Michigan, and Virginia, along with those from Canada, France (of course), Argentina, Australia, and New Zealand. That is not quite the whole of the Pinot world—I've had nice wines from Chile, Italy, and South Africa, for example, and there's also Richard Leakey's Kenyan Pinot Noir—but it is enough to fully engage most people over a long weekend in July. The Grand Seminar (and it really is grand) in 2016 featured a Master Class on Australian Pinot Noir. Michael Hill Smith MW was one of the speakers and his Tasmanian Tolpuddle Pinot a featured wine. Events like IPNC are not inexpensive to produce nor cheap to attend, but they offer a range of experiences that, if you can get deeper than the pure hedonism of the dinners and tastings, help us understand something about global wine and how it is changing.[1]

WELCOME TO PLANET RIESLING

If you time it right, you can celebrate Pinot Noir in Oregon and then motor up the highway to rendezvous with Planet Riesling in Seattle, which is this chapter's destination. Riesling Rendezvous happens every three years (Germany and Australia host Riesling gatherings in the interstitial years) and it differs from the IPNC in many ways. The wines are different and most of the people, too, but so is the focus. Yes there is a Grand Tasting on Sunday on the beautiful grounds of Chateau Ste. Michelle in Woodinville, but the next two days are aimed squarely at winemakers, wine media, and the wine trade. Consumer enthusiasts are welcome, but the agenda is strictly business. The 2016 edition featured wineries from Washington, Oregon, California, Idaho, Michigan, and New York, along with Australia, Austria, Canada, France, Germany (of course), and New Zealand. The trade and media participants came from far and wide as well.

Riesling Rendezvous is organized by Washington State's Chateau Ste. Michelle, the world's largest producer of Riesling wines, and Germany's Dr. Loosen. Ernst Loosen, whom I admire a lot, is perhaps the world's foremost, most enthusiastic, and hardest-working proponent of Riesling wine. It is no surprise that a Mosel Valley producer would be behind a global gathering like this, but the Washington State link might catch a lot of people off guard. Washington State—isn't it cold and wet? Not sure they can even grow grapes there, much less make wine. Yes, yes, I know, because I live in these parts. In fact it is an old joke among local winemakers that when they tell outsiders about wine in Washington they are met with a moment of silence and then the inevitable question, "Oh, which side of the Potomac is your vineyard on?" Potomac? Ah yes, they are thinking of the *other Washington*—Washington, D.C.

The fact is that Seattle (think Boeing, Starbucks, Amazon.com, and grunge music) is on the wet west side of the state where ocean weather systems dominate, but most of the vineyards are east of the Cascade Mountain range, which wrings all the moisture out of the Pacific's clouds, leaving a huge rain shadow. The Columbia Valley is accordingly a dry place where agriculture thrives because of the sunny weather and usually plentiful irrigation water. A variety of fascinating vineyard *terroirs* have been discovered here in the last fifty years as the region's rich geological legacy (which involves rivers, glaciers, volcanoes, and a massive Ice Age event called the Great Missoula Flood) have been explored.

Chateau Ste. Michelle was one of Washington's post-Prohibition pioneers. Their big vineyard investments in the 1970s and 1980s helped jump-start the Washington industry, which is now second only to California in the United States. Washington became known for its Rieslings early on and its international reputation has grown. Two noteworthy international collaborations have resulted: Ernst Loosen makes a line of Washington Riesling called Eroica in partnership with Chateau Ste. Michelle, while Armin Diel of German Riesling producer Schlossgut Diel makes a Washington wine called Poet's Leap with the Long Shadows winery near Walla Walla. Eroica and Poet's Leap are often on the short list of best American Rieslings and best wines in general. No wonder Riesling producers from around the world are happy to come here to talk business.

WHAT DO YOU DO AT A RIESLING RENDEZVOUS?

So what happens at a Riesling Rendezvous? I hope you won't be disappointed if I tell you that a lot of time is spent drinking (or tasting and spitting) Riesling wines. All the winemakers bring wines and for many of them the opportunity to taste wines from around the world is as important as all the speakers and seminars combined. Winemakers talk a lot about the perils of "cellar palate," which is the problem that occurs when you spend all your time tasting your own wines (or reading your own books, in my case). There is no substitute for tasting the other person's wines and seeing what they are up to and how your wines measure up. There is no way to overstate how valuable this is and it helps explain why winemakers will spend thousands of dollars to fly themselves and their wines to these conference to share in exchange for the chance to learn from others. Serious business!

The conference organizers acknowledge this function by staging the event around two rather intimidating formal tastings. You walk into the conference hall on the first morning and there are twenty glasses arrayed in front of each of the three hundred places. You are about to spend more than two hours tasting twenty dry Riesling wines "blind" (without knowing who made them, when, or where). One by one, the wines are discussed and the identities revealed. Twenty off-dry and sweeter wines are tasted this way on the second day. It is quite an incredible experience and, from a logistical standpoint, a lot of wines to wrangle and a lot of wineglasses to set out, fill, dump, and collect.

Understanding *terroir* and learning from the European masters seemed to be high on the list of priorities when I attended my first Rendezvous in 2008. The wines from the Nahe River Valley in Germany were particularly noteworthy, especially the Weingut Dönnhoff Niederhäuser Hermannshöle Auslese, which just seemed to dance in my glass. What a wine! A highlight for me was a seminar where wine importer Terry Theise led us on a journey across the Demeter-certified biodynamic vineyards of one of Austria's oldest wineries, Nikolaihof Wachau. The wines we tasted included the Nikolaihof Riesling Steiner Hund Reserve, if memory serves. It was an intense experience—I actually had to leave the room a couple of times to catch my breath. But I kept coming back because the intellectual and sensory experiences were so overwhelming.[2]

Dönnhoff and Nikolaihof still stood out the next time around, but I found myself drawn to Riesling's dry side. I met Louisa Rose, who makes the spectacular Eden Valley Pewsey Vale The Contours Riesling for Yalumba in Australia, for example, and savored several vintages of Trimbach Riesling Cuvée Frédéric Émile from Alsace. It was clear that Riesling is not just off-dry or sweet but could also be bone dry and delicious. And Planet Riesling, as Stuart Pigott calls it, extends beyond the tight German-Austrian orbit.

I have noticed that there is a certain amount of talking in circles that takes place during these tastings. The same issues seem to come up over and over again. Do you *really* think this is a *dry* Riesling (often stated as an accusation more than a question)? Soon the focus shifts to the analytical data (RS, residual sugar; TA, total acidity; pH, acid/alkaline balance), which is another set of circles to probe and debate. Then the big question: Is this Old World or New World? It is as if each wine must fit neatly into an objective category and, of course, they don't.

These debates seem like a dead end to me. Perception of sweet and dry is individual and subjective, so what is dry to you might be sweet to someone else. The analytical data have limited significance, as Jamie Goode, who also attended the 2016 meetings, explained.[3] And it doesn't matter to me very much if someone can guess where the wine is from—wine should not be a game of "Where in the World is Carmen Sandiego." In any case, even the experts usually couldn't answer the Old/New geography question with confidence and there were many surprises when makers and regions were revealed.

You might have enjoyed the scene at the two formal tastings in 2013. Sometimes the experts were spot on when they offered their best guesses about what was in the glass, but I think the organizers might have selected the lineup of wines to make the point that Planet Riesling is changing. So sometimes (more often than not, I believe) they were fooled. Fooled, generally, by unexpected quality from an unexpected source, which is a nice way to be surprised.

There were ooohs and aaahs, for example, when one wine was revealed to be from Elesko Winery in Slovakia. Wow, none of us saw that coming, probably because we didn't have Slovakia on our radar in the first place. I remember tasting a few crisp, delicious white wines from this region when I taught in Prague, but beer, not wine, is probably the first thing that comes to mind (despite Austria's obvious proximity) when you think Central Europe. Very impressive.

Tim Atkin, who moderated the off-dry tasting (John Winthrop Haeger handled the job for the dry wines[4]) seemed to take special pleasure in revealing that a wine that had been firmly placed in the Mosel region by an expert panelist was in fact made by Ste. Chapelle of Idaho (part of the rapidly rising Precept Wine group). How many cases do you make, Atkin asked winemaker Maureen Johnson, probably imagining a sort of small-potatoes Idaho wine industry? Forty thousand cases of this wine, came the reply. Wow, that's lot, Atkin said, obviously surprised. Huge by German standards. It's a brave new world on Planet Riesling when fine wines can come from such unexpected corners of the globe.

This message was reinforced in Stuart Pigott's 2014 book, *Best White Wine on Earth: The Riesling Story.*[5] Although Pigott dutifully (and enthusiastically) surveys all of Planet Riesling's regions and styles, it is not insignificant that he seems to sense that the New World represents the future, both in terms of rising production and especially potential consumption. It is not enough, after all, to make great wine. Someone needs to drink it. And that can be a problem.

RIESLING'S IDENTITY CRISIS

One constant theme of these meetings is the need to overcome Riesling's identity crisis. What's the problem with Riesling? Well, the issue is that most consumers misunderstand Riesling and the problems usually start with sweetness. Rieslings come in all shades of sweet, from not sweet—as dry as you can get—all the way over to intensely sweet (if usually balanced by acidity). What you think of Riesling may be determined by your first sip, and for many people that sip was uncomfortably sweet (especially if you weren't expecting it). So Riesling (like sherry, another misunderstood wine) is held to be guilty of criminal sweetness until proven innocent. And many consumers, convinced by what they have heard or believe, never give it a fair trial. Even worse in a way is the fact that some people who *like* sweeter wines are confused when they chance upon a dry Riesling. Is that Riesling? Not what I expected. Consumers are often afraid to buy Riesling because they can't tell what they are going to get when they open the bottle. The "how sweet *is* it?" question and the "how sweet it *is*" exclamation (of those who know the answer) are thus inextricably linked.

Students of economics will recognize this as a problem of asymmetric information. The people who make wine know its flavor profile and the people who buy it presumably know what they like (although winemakers tell me that people tend to *say* they like dry Riesling, but end up buying sweeter products). But they don't know what's in the bottle and can only find out by trying it. One answer to the asymmetric information trap is signaling: tell the buyers what they need to know to make a purchase with confidence. It sounds pretty simple, but most Riesling makers have until recently resisted it, possibly because they didn't want to alienate one side or the other in the sweetness wars. The simple graphic sweetness scale created by the International Riesling Foundation (an organization that came out of the first Rendezvous meeting) certainly helps and more producers are now using it.

Research presented at the 2013 conference suggests one more problem. The people who love Riesling the most (perhaps because they appreciate its diversity) apparently also appreciate the diversity of wine generally. They drink Riesling, of course, but not with the single-minded resolve of, for example, Sauvignon Blanc or Pinot Grigio fans, who come back more frequently to their favorite wine than do Riesling's core consumer group.

So how do you get consumers to buy wines that they don't completely understand or fully appreciate? Well, perhaps predictably the discussion turned early on to the idea of a cool motto—the "Got Milk?" killer tagline for their respective wines. This always seems to happen when wine people get together to talk category marketing, despite the fact that there are darn few generic marketing slogans that have had much impact on sales (how many can you think of?) and even fewer when it comes to wine. I used to think that this discussion was simply a waste of time, but now I recognize that the function is not so much to bring in consumers as to give wineries and distributors a rallying cry. No harm in that, so long as the slogan isn't offensive, and it might even be useful. Chateau Ste. Michelle CEO Ted Baseler proposed "Right On, Riesling!" and that seems fine—certainly better than the vaguely suggestive "Riesling: Just Put It In Your Mouth" that one breakout group played with for a while.

There isn't any one way to build a market for a misunderstood or underappreciated wine—no silver bullet, as we say in the U.S. There must be fifty ways (or five hundred), but they all seem to boil down to hard work that is done one glass and one consumer at a time (leveraged by whatever peer-to-peer social media effects you can muster and of course beneficial media attention). Unite behind whatever rallying cry works for you, residents of Planet Riesling, because there really is strength in numbers, and get on to the hard work.

THE MOTHER OF ALL COMMON ENEMIES

Nothing unites competitors like a common challenge (like convincing consumers to give Riesling a try) except maybe a common enemy and Riesling Rendezvous has identified a potentially unstoppable collective threat. Not phylloxera or some other vine disease this time or even the neo-prohibition movement that is so active in Europe these days. This enemy is as big as Mother Nature: climate change.

Climate change has been reshaping Planet Riesling for some time. Ernst Loosen started noticing the changes in his Mosel vineyards a good while ago and told Jancis Robinson back in 2008 that his best sites were now ripening so well that it was nearly impossible to produce the traditional Kabinett-style dry wines there.[6] Sure enough, when I bought some bottles of Loosen Blue Slate Riesling for a student tasting, I saw on the back label a notice that it wasn't clear how much longer this wine could be made. So perhaps it was not a coincidence that the 2010 edition of Riesling Rendezvous featured a presentation on climate change by Hans Schultz of Geisenheim University (where they have been collecting vineyard weather data for hundreds of years) and Gregory V. Jones of Southern Oregon University. (If you drove up Interstate 5 at the start of the chapter you passed pretty close to his family's Abacela Winery in Southern Oregon.)

I remember the Schultz and Jones presentation in 2010 very well because it had some shocking news. They presented climate-change forecasts for 2025 that had been made in around 2000 and compared them with recent data. Actual global warming had already hit the 2025 forecasts in 2010, 15 years too soon. And, as we know from previous chapters, temperatures have been higher each year since then. Riesling is a relatively adaptable grape variety, which can produce quality fruit with average growing season temperatures from about 13°C to 17°C. But there are limits even for noble Riesling.

Schultz and Jones's 2016 presentation took the audience beyond the issue of rising temperatures. Yes the daily peak temperatures have been rising in many winegrowing regions, they noted, but the growing-season low temperatures have been rising, too, often faster than the peak highs. Why does this matter? Well, it is an article of faith among many winemakers that the key to crisp, ripe wines lies in the diurnal variation—the difference between the heat of the day and the cool of the night during growing season. The heat ripens and sweetens, but the cool preserves the acidity needed to balance the wines. If, as the research suggests, the diurnal gap is shrinking, then the balance that it is thought to create is changing, too, and may require adjustments in winegrowing and winemaking practices.

Soil temperature is another factor that is changing, according to Schultz and Jones. Some studies that monitored the soil temperature at different depths below the vineyard surface found higher readings, which makes sense when you think about it but still comes as a surprise. Higher soil temperatures potentially impact how the plants develop both in general and over the course of the season. Significantly, some studies suggest that what we think of as differences due to *terroir* are actually associated with the microbes that inhabit the soil. The changing soil environment may therefore alter the grapes and wine in subtle but fundamental ways. The audience was both shaken and stirred by the Schultz and Jones presentation and you could see them trying to process all the detailed information and thinking about what it meant for their vineyards, grapes, wines, and businesses.

ON THE RIESLING ROAD

So there is very good news on Planet Riesling in terms of the quality of the wines today, but there are still challenges to address starting with the common enemy that is climate change. There is much work to be done in building the market, too. Just because consumers understand that Riesling comes in many different styles of levels of sweetness, this doesn't mean that they will buy it. No one has to drink Riesling. No one has to drink wine at all. There are many other wines and other beverages and each product must make its case to potential buyers every day. As I wrote in *The Wine Economist* after Riesling Rendezvous 2016, I am a bit concerned that Planet Riesling is stuck talking in circles—dry versus sweet, Old World versus New World—when the market has moved on.

I find inspiration, however, in something Ernst Loosen said on the first day of the conference. Riesling is complicated, he observed, and complicated things need to be understood in complicated ways (does this remind you of Batali's Impossibility Theorem?). Exactly, but how do you get that message across? Well, in my other life as a university professor writing about economic globalization I learned that people understand complicated things through the stories that we tell about them.[7] The stories need to be carefully crafted so that they capture the essence without oversimplifying or distorting. Storytelling is the key and that's Riesling's challenge, which means going beyond the simply dichotomies that sometimes dominate the discussion.

So which wines should we add to our collection? Since much of the Riesling wine world has come to meet us in Seattle I am going to choose a range of wine styles from all over the map. I'll start on the dry side with Pewsey Vales The Contours Eden Valley Riesling from Australia and Tantalus Old Vines Riesling Okanagan Valley from British Columbia, Canada. Then we move to off-dry styles with Dr. Loosen & Chateau Ste. Michelle Eroica Riesling Columbia Valley, Washington, and Weingut Dönnhoff Niederhäuser Hermannshöle Auslese, Nahe Valley, Germany.

～

The Wines

Pewsey Vales The Contours Riesling, Eden Valley, Australia

Tantalus Old Vines Riesling Okanagan Valley, British Columbia, Canada

Dr. Loosen and Chateau Ste. Michelle Eroica Riesling, Columbia Valley, Washington

Weingut Dönnhoff Niederhäuser Hermannshöle Auslese, Nahe Valley, Germany

～

Chapter 15

Cannonball Run

The Cannonball Run is the title of a ridiculous 1981 film that starred a long list of actors and celebrities beginning with Burt Reynolds, Roger Moore, Farrah Fawcett, Dom DeLuise, Sammy Davis, Jr., and Dean Martin, and continuing down the line with Jackie Chan, Peter Fonda, Bianca Jagger, Molly Picon, Mel Tillis, Terry Bradshaw, Bert Convy, and Jimmy "The Greek" Snyder. If you don't recognize these names, then I guess you weren't around in the 1980s. Trust me, this is a who's who of eighties American popular culture. No wonder this film was a box-office hit and spawned (is that the right word?) a 1984 sequel predictably titled *Cannonball Run II*. At this writing there are rumors that Warner Bros. film studio is planning to revive the franchise. Can't wait.

Somewhere pretty far down on the list of stars you will find the name of automotive writer Brock Yates, who also authored the screenplay and invented, more or less, the real life adventure on which the film is based. Brock Yates's Cannonball Run was a totally illegal no-holds-barred automobile race across North America on public roads and highways starting at the Atlantic and ending at the Portofino Inn in Redondo Beach, California.[1] It was run five times in the 1970s. American racing legend Dan Gurney won the second race driving a Ferrari Daytona with Brock Yates riding shotgun in a time of thirty-two hours fifty-four minutes. The best official race time was set by Dave Heinz in 1979: thirty-two hours fifty-one minutes in a Jaguar XJS. Since then others have recreated the run on their own, eventually pushing the quickest unofficial time to less than thirty hours.[2]

The thing about the Cannonball Run is that it has always reminded me of Phileas Fogg's desperate dash (in the opposite direction) across the vast continent. Fogg's steam locomotive was, like the popular film's souped-up cars, the fastest form of conventional transit on public thoroughfares. Time was the enemy in both cases and carefully laid plans were shredded in dramatic fashion (for Fogg) and ludicrous ways (the film). It is time for us to make a Cannonball Run of our own.

BURSTING AT THE SEAMS

California is by far the largest wine-producing region in North America. *Wine Business Monthly* calculated that there were 2,885 bonded wineries in the state in 2016 and 1,169 "virtual" wineries (marketing brands made under contract by others), for a total of 4,054 wine producers in California, including most of the thirty largest producers.[3] There is no doubt: California is Number One. But there is a lot more to American wine than California. Incredibly, there were more than 8,700 wineries in the United States in 2016 plus more than 670 in Canada. Mexico is experiencing a wine boom, too. There are more than one hundred wineries in Baja California, Mexico alone, no surprise given that the Spanish introduced wine grapes there centuries ago.

Wine was made in every U.S. state in 2016, with California followed by Washington with 718 wineries, Oregon (689), New York (367), Virginia (262), and Texas (228).[4] So many wineries! What should we do—travel to every state and province and visit every winery we can? We could do that, but it would take forever—literally forever, I think, because by the time we finished there would be more new wineries to visit. *Wine Business Monthly* says that the number of U.S. wineries increased by more than 700 in 2015 alone. Amazing! America is bursting at the seams with wine and wineries.

It would take an entire book just to scratch the surface of American wine. Fortunately that volume exists: *American Wine*, a beautiful and informative 2013 book by Jancis Robinson and Linda Murphy.[5] One of the things that I like best about *American Wine* is that it takes its title seriously. You would expect the major producing states like California, Washington, New York, and Oregon to get detailed treatment here and they do. But you might not expect detailed analysis of Colorado, for example, with its rapidly emerging industry, or Missouri with its important viticultural history. Indeed, every state makes wine in one way or another and every state gets consideration here. Alabama and Mississippi get just a paragraph each, it must be said, but maybe that's not a surprise.

American Wine helped me reimagine America as a country where wine is deeply embedded in history and culture and widely embraced. Although the United States is the largest wine market in the world measured by total sales, per capita wine consumption is still low in America if we judge by European standards, and wine still struggles to overcome the regulatory legacy of Prohibition. *American Wine* recognizes these challenges, but it projects an inspiring vision of wine today that suggests how it might evolve and develop in the future.

Fortified by this vision, let's start our Cannonball Run across North America's wine landscape, stopping at a few places that have particular stories to tell. I warn you that this is going to be a bit fragmented as we lurch and pivot from place to place, but there is no practical alternative. To make it interesting, let's have a race. Half of us will take a northern route and the rest head south, so that we cover twice as much territory. Where shall we meet? I know! Let's aim for the Palladio Restaurant in Barboursville, Virginia. I'll explain when we get there. Now . . . start your engines.

NORTHERN EXPOSURE

We are headed to Canada first, which will surprise many people. Canada? Really? Tundra red and Tundra white? No, but they do make ice wine in both Ontario and British Columbia. The grapes are left on the vine until the temperature dips low enough to freeze the juice. Then the icy, shriveled grapes are pressed, yielding just a few drops of nectar that ferments into a deliciously sweet wine that is Canada's most important wine export.

I was fortunate to be invited to give keynote speeches to both the Ontario and British Columbia wine industry groups in 2015, so I had an opportunity to taste many of their best wines. Ontario has a bigger wine industry than you might think—looking at a map will tell you why. Ontario dips down around the Great Lakes and part of the province is as far south as the Willamette Valley in Oregon. Why shouldn't they make good wine? Climate change is a challenge, however. Not warming so much as instability. Unexpected movements in the jet stream in recent years have made Ontario's winelands unusually frigid in the winter months. Although much of the Ontario wine industry is focused on inexpensive wines, some of which are blended with imported bulk wine and marketed as Canada-international blends, there is a growing quality movement devoted to VQA (Vintners Quality Alliance) wines. One of my Ontario favorites (which I previously enjoyed at a Riesling Rendezvous gathering) is the Cave Springs Cellars Estate Riesling from the Beamsville Bench on the Niagara Peninsula.

I love the Rieslings from British Columbia, too (perhaps you noticed that I included the Tantalus Old Vines Riesling in the last chapter's wine list), but it was the reds that I discovered when I spoke there in 2015. I have been visiting B.C. for many years and the wines have improved so much. Climate change, I asked one winemaker? He was insulted. No, he said, it is better winemaking, and I am sure that is true as it is in so many parts of the world. But apparently economics is also part of the answer. When Canada entered the North American Free Trade Agreement (NAFTA), its wine market opened up a bit wider to U.S. wines and this forced B.C. wineries to upgrade their vineyards, many of which had previously been planted with hybrid grapes. The new *Vitis vinifera* vines took a while to take hold, but when they did they produced some excellent fruit and these days some red wines to go along with the whites. The C.C. Jentsch Cellars Okanagan Valley Syrah is one example of what can be achieved here. Howard Soon, who is probably Canada's most-awarded winemaker, crafts a series of outstanding single-vineyard red wines for his Sandhill winery that probe British Columbia's relatively under-explored wine *terroirs*. Soon's Sandhill One is a complex Bordeaux-style blend of Cabernet Sauvignon, Petit Verdot, and Malbec from the Phantom Creek Vineyard that proves once and for all that Canada is more than ice wine.

WALLA WALLA COMES OF AGE

Now we veer south a bit to Walla Walla, which has a surprisingly long wine history. We think the first grapes were planted by French-Canadian trappers who came here with the Hudson's Bay Company about two hundred years ago. Italian immigrants were serious about grapes and wine when they came after the Civil War. One of the grape varieties they favored was Cinsault, which they called the "Black Prince." Some of their vines are still here growing wild, but harvested by someone. You will make people here smile if you ask for their Cinsault or mention the Black Prince.

We were up on a hilltop on the Oregon side of the AVA for a festive dinner at the Glass House of the Caderetta vineyard, where we tasted a number of local Bordeaux blend wines with the meal. Marty Clubb of the Walla Walla pioneer winery L'Ecole No. 41 was there and we tasted his 2011 Ferguson Vineyard blend.[6] I think we could actually see the recently developed Ferguson Vineyard over the hill from our vantage point. The wine was great, with a real sense of place and Marty told us that he was about to fly off to London because of this wine. The L'Ecole team was so happy with the Ferguson that they had entered it in the *Decanter* World Wine Awards and he had been summoned to London for the awards dinner.

The invitation meant that the wine had won one of the bigger prizes—not just a bronze, silver, or gold. Maybe a regional trophy (best U.S. Bordeaux varietal wine?) or maybe even an International Trophy (best of all the wine in this category from all over the world!). No way to tell which it was, but Marty was willing to fly to London to find out. How exciting! A couple of days later I was busy hitting the F5 reload key on my laptop, impatient to see the *Decanter* results appear on my screen. And finally at 1:01 pm there they were. L'Ecole won the Decanter International Trophy for Best Bordeaux Varietal Red Wine over £15—the top global award in one of the most competitive wine categories.

Winning a *Decanter* award or any other prize or medal obviously doesn't prove that one particular wine is objectively "better" (whatever that means) than any other. But, I would argue, it is hard to deny that the excellence of the L'Ecole Ferguson stood out to the initial American tasting panel, which is how it entered in the International Trophy competition. And it obviously stood out there, too, when tasted with similar wines from other parts of the world. Not rocket science, I agree, but still worth celebrating. Best in the world? That's a matter of opinion. But a sign that Walla Walla has come of age? Absolutely yes! So many great wines are being made in this region now and the future is bright. Some of my favorites are the Corliss Syrah, Reininger Carmenère, Pepper Bridge Trine, and the Tranche Chardonnay, which is made from grapes grown at the Celilo Vineyard in the Columbia Gorge area.

ON THE ROAD AGAIN

From Walla Walla we head east through Idaho (which had fifty-one wineries in 2016), where many fine wines are produced, especially in the Snake River Valley area. This is where that surprising Ste. Chapelle Riesling we encountered in the last chapter was made. I am very fond of the red wines of Huston Vineyards, including the easy-drinking Chicken Dinner Red, and all the wines that Greg Koenig makes for his Koenig Winery, Bittner Winery, and others.

Then it is on to Montana (sixteen wineries), South Dakota (twenty-two wineries), and then Minnesota (sixty-two wineries). The University of Minnesota has worked to develop wine grapes that will thrive in northern latitudes. One of these is Frontenac, a hybrid grape variety created in 1978 by combining Landot Noir and a vine discovered growing wild near Jordan, Minnesota. The wines are deep red, with flavors of plum and cherry. I have twice tasted a wine called Voyageur made with this grape from Alexis Bailly Vineyard. One vintage of Voyageur was named the "best wine made in America" at an Atlanta wine competition.

Our northern route continues through winegrowing states including Michigan, where some wonderful wines can be found near Traverse City, including some stunning Rieslings. Ohio is noteworthy both for its current winegrowing boom and for its interesting history. Nicholas Longworth (1782–1863) dreamed of an America full of vines and wines and he identified Ohio in general and Cincinnati in particular as its potential center.[7] He retired from business in 1828 and set about building a new world of wine based primarily around the Catawba grape variety. He was audaciously ambitious and I think he would have succeeded were it not for the various diseases that plagued his effort and that caused his precious grapevines (and his dreams) to wither and die.

New York, with both the Finger Lakes and Long Island wine regions, is home to a dynamic wine scene along with surprising New Jersey.[8] The Boordy Vineyards in Maryland has both good wine and historical importance.[9] We have skipped over hundreds of wineries and thousands of wines, but we made it here to Virginia. How did the other group do?

DESERT WINE?

The image that comes to mind when you think of a vineyard is lush and green, not dusty desert tan. But the reality is that some important winegrowing regions feature near-desert conditions. I'm thinking of parts of Ningxia in China, for example, and Mendoza, Argentina, although I could name several more. So it shouldn't be a surprise that grapes are grown and wine is made in the American southwest. We visited wineries in the Sonoita region of Arizona, a short drive from Tucson, and found some exceptional wines at Dos Cabezas WineWorks and Callaghan Vineyards.

New Mexico doesn't seem like a place where you would find much wine. Chiles, yes, especially the chiles from Hatch, which are famous among fans of Southwest cuisine. But wine? Probably not. And yet it was near Socorro, New Mexico, in 1629 that a Franciscan father planted the first grapevines in what is now the United States, and there are now forty-nine wineries in the state. One of them has a most unusual story.

Members of the Gruet family of Gruet et Fils, a French Champagne house, were vaguely searching for vineyard opportunities when they were passing through the American Southwest in 1983. They ran into some fellow European winemakers who were trying to make a go of it in New Mexico and, inspired by their example, ended up planting vineyards at elevation 4,300 feet near the town of Truth or Consequences, about 170 miles south of Albuquerque. The winery equipment was shipped over from France along with members of the Gruet family to make the wine and, in due course, a first vintage (1987) was released. Today Gruet produces a full range of sparkling wine and some still wines, too. Wine from New Mexico? What a nice surprise. And they taste great with food, even with blue corn enchiladas with (Hatch) green chile sauce.

Texas has become a booming wine state with more than 225 wineries and counting. Texans are proud of their wines and like them so much that some of the wineries bring in grapes from California to supplement what the local vineyards can produce, leading to something of a controversy about what a "Texas" wine really is. Oklahoma has caught wine fever, too, with more than fifty wineries so far.

MISSOURI WAS THE FIRST

We could have paused in Missouri on either our northern or southern journey, but since the main vineyard area is in the south part of the state, that's our next stop. Missouri had 135 wineries at last count, which will probably surprise even the people who live in the "show me" state. More surprising still, however, is the fact that a Missouri wine region—Augusta, just west of St. Louis—was the very first American Viticultural Area. The Augusta AVA was approved in June 1980, eight months before the second AVA, which we visited a couple of chapters ago: Napa Valley. I associate Missouri with its signature hybrid grape variety, Norton, which was discovered in 1820 by Richmond, Virginia, physician and horticulturalist Daniel Norton and is the mainstay of the wine industry here in Missouri.

Time to speed on through North Carolina, which is quickly emerging as a wine region that might someday rival Virginia. North Carolina features both European *Vitis vinifera* grape varieties and the native *Vitis rotundifolia* Muscadine grapes, including Scuppernong. These grapes do well in hot, humid climates, according to *American Wine,* and are made into popular sweetish wines throughout the American South.[10] Wines made from native grape varieties (including Nicholas Longworth's Catawba wines) have a "foxy" flavor that is an honest if acquired taste.

Wine is not everywhere in America, but that seems to be where it is headed, and we need to move on and pay homage to an American who dreamed that one day this would happen. And so we cross the border into Thomas Jefferson's Virginia.

THOMAS JEFFERSON'S LEGACY

Thomas Jefferson famously fell in love with wine when he was minister to France (succeeding Benjamin Franklin) from 1785 to 1789. America was quite familiar with wine in those days, but madeira was the standard, not the dry wines of Burgundy or Bordeaux. Jefferson was taken by French wine and had cases sent home, and he eventually took the next step by sending grapevines themselves. Why shouldn't the New World make and enjoy great Old World–style wines? The answer, as you might guess from Nicolas Longworth's later experiment in Ohio, was disease and probably also the phylloxera louse. Jefferson's dream was not realized in his lifetime, but it is happening today, both in Virginia, which now boasts more than 260 wineries, and across the country, too.

Our Cannonball Run journey ends at the Palladio Restaurant at Barboursville Vineyards, only a few miles from Jefferson's Monticello. The Barboursville estate itself dates to Jefferson's time. James Barbour was a governor of

Virginia and Jefferson designed the buildings in what is called a neo-Palladian style that he also used for Monticello, the University of Virginia, and the Virginia State Capitol building in Richmond. Jefferson's taste in wine might have leaned French, but his passion for architecture was inspired by Italy and the classic lines of Andrea Palladio in particular.

It might have been fate that guided Gianni Zonin to Barboursville and its heritage in the 1970s. Zonin is an important wine-producing family in Italy and Gianni was looking to establish an outpost in the United States. Zonin went on a sort of Cannonball Run of his own, surveying the prospects for wine investment in California and various other U.S. regions. His search ended here in Jefferson country, where he saw the possibilities that were invisible to others on the old Barboursville estate. And so, in the American bicentennial year 1976, they planted grapevines and created a winery and the wonderful Palladio restaurant, where Sue and I hosted a family luncheon in honor of her parents Mike and Gert Trbovich who live nearby in Richmond.

We met with winemaker Luca Paschina before lunch to taste through the wines, which are generally ranked among Virginia's best (the Reserve Petit Verdot won the Monticello Cup in 2016). There was much delight as we sipped the vibrant Vermentino Reserve and the Cabernet Franc, which is my personal reference point for this variety in Virginia. Then Luca, who is originally from Piemonte in northern Italy, poured his Nebbiolo Reserve. "Wow!" Sue's brother Alan was both taken and taken aback by this wine. I was surprised, too. The conventional wisdom is that Nebbiolo doesn't do very well outside Piemonte. Is there much fog around here, I asked Alan, who lives down the road near the University of Virginia campus? Lots of fog, he replied. Interesting—*nebbia* means fog in Italian. Maybe that's why the wine was so good in its own distinct Virginia way.

The final wine was Barboursville's flagship, Octagon, a Bordeaux-style blend made in Jefferson's honor and featuring the architect's drawing of the estate's Octagon Room on the label. A perfect tribute to Jefferson's vision. Octagon was great, but really all of the wines were memorable. Which should go into our eighty-bottle case? I had the opportunity to ask this question to Domenico Zonin, now head of the family firm, when I spoke at a conference organized by the Unione Italiana Vini in Milan. Which Barboursville wine? Octagon, of course, he said. Yes, I agreed, but what about the Nebbiolo? Doesn't that also say something special about Virginia and the Italy-Virginia connection (and about the winemaker, Luca Paschina, too)? Yes, Zonin replied, the Nebbiolo is special. And so is Barboursville Vineyards.

THE WINES

Choosing the wines is always difficult, especially for this part of our journey. Impossible to select all the great wines, so we must settle for just a few that tell a story. Barboursville, of course, because of Jefferson and the Zonin connection, but which one? The Octagon? Or the Nebbiolo Reserve? Easy answer: both. Let me add just one more before we jump in our dusty rental car and head off for Dulles International Airport to catch the evening British Air flight to Heathrow. I have to include the L'Ecole No. 41 Ferguson red blend that won the *Decanter* prize and demonstrates that American wine beyond California has the quality to shine on the global stage.

With that, our grand global Cannonball Run is almost over. A few hours in the air and we will complete our journey. After all this time and all these wines, did we succeed in our quest or did we come up short? What do you think? Only one way to find out.

~

The Wines

L'Ecole 41 Ferguson Vineyard, Walla Walla, Washington

Barboursville Vineyards Nebbiolo Reserve, Virginia

Barboursville Vineyards Octagon, Virginia

~

Chapter 16

Back to London

Victory! Or Defeat?

Phileas Fogg arrived in London a defeated man. The journey had taken too long. Too many unexpected delays, missed connections, unlucky twists of fate. So close. Just a few hours earlier and he would have celebrated victory. But a miss is as good as a mile when the stakes are so high. He had lost the twenty-thousand-pound wager—a fortune! Even worse, he had spent nearly that much again to make the journey. Double doom!

But it was not Phileas Fogg's fate to die a sad pauper. As readers of Jules Verne's novel will remember, he is saved by a classic plot twist that I will not reveal here except to hint that it has something to do with the fact that he had been traveling west to east all around the world and that direction has a way of distorting the information that Passepartout's ridiculously reliable watch— set steadfast to London time—reported each day.

Instead of a day late, they are exactly on time! Victory is unexpectedly rescued from defeat and at the last minute, too. What a wonderful way to end a novel. How will *our* journey end? Victory? Or defeat?

THE FINISH LINE

And so here we are once again at 3 Saint James's Street in London, just down the road from Fogg's finish line at the Reform Club. What better place to assess our journey than where it began, on the wine-filled premises of Berry Bros. & Rudd?

Our challenge was not to collect the most wines or even necessarily the best wines—there are lots of buyer's guides and critic reports to help with that. Rather, we were guided by the admittedly imprecise directive to choose wines that tell a story. Individually and then as a group, our choices are required to "represent" the world of wine, its people and culture, and tell us why wine has been so such an object of enjoyment, fascination, passion, and even obsession. That's a lot to ask—maybe too much?—and the final "why wine?" verdict is sure to be contested.

We have covered a lot of territory. We have tasted some of the finest and most sought-after wines on earth, wines so sublime that they are treasured and even valued like works of fine art. Château Petrus, Kanonkop Pinotage, Penfolds Grange, Henschke Hill of Grace, Stag's Leap Wine Cellars Cabernet, and many others in our case are simply sublime and tasting them is often a once-in-a-lifetime experience. Wow! If we were seeking stories of wine at its finest, I think we have a collection that represents that idea very well even if there are inevitable omissions.

But there is more to wine than this iconic tier. The works of the great authors are like fine wine, Mark Twain once said, mine are like water. Everyone drinks water. So we have also tasted the wines of the people, since they are important, too. As a fan of Mark Twain, I cannot ignore the wines of the people like Mateus Rosé, Four Cousins, and Two-Buck Chuck. And if these wines are not always the same transforming experience as the world's most treasured wines, the comfort and enjoyment they provide and their ability facilitate conversation, friendship, even love, should not be underestimated. They are part of the "why wine?" answer, too.

We have found a few wines that tell exceptional stories about the human spirit. Richard Leakey's Kenyan Pinot Noir, for example, or the wines of war and peace from Château Musar in Lebanon. Leakey's wine is essentially impossible to taste, so its story will have to inspire us on its own, but Château Musar wines are available in major markets and are not as expensive as you might suppose. They are a tribute to Serge Hochar's optimistic determination that can lift us up even in the darkest moments and teach us about natural wine's battle against industrialization, too.

Inevitably we have become embroiled in serious controversy. Burgundy or Bordeaux? The choice is not just about the grape variety or the shape of the bottle. It is also about a whole vision of what wine is or should be. The same can be said in a different context about the selection of *terroir*-driven Hill of Grace or winemaker-determined Grange. Tasmania reminded us that wine is inescapably a product of nature and nature is on the move. Climate change, which we encountered again at the Riesling Rendezvous, is one of wine's (and society's) greatest challenges. Why wine? Because it has so much to teach us about our world.

Sailing across the South Pacific from Tasmania to New Zealand to South American was more than just an opportunity to view the Southern Cross. Each of the wine regions we visited had a story to tell about love, life, loss, and what endures. Wine must be a very special thing to survive crisis and renew itself in so many ways.

Our Cannonball Run across North America went by so fast that the individual stories got a bit blurred at times, but the big story came through pretty clearly. Jefferson dreamed of an America where wine was made, consumed, loved, and appreciated. It took a couple of hundred years, but eventually the natural obstacles like phylloxera and human hurdles like Prohibition have been overcome if not entirely conquered. America, like Walla Walla, which I used to represent it, is coming of age as a wine country.

Looking back, it is easy to see that we have taken more than a few shortcuts, which I suppose was inevitable. France, Italy, and Spain together produce more than half of all the wine in the world, so it would make sense if they made up half of our eighty wines and an equal share of the stories, but they did not, in order to make room for others. Each of the wine world's Big Three was featured in a chapter, but they are still vastly underrepresented relative to their place in the vino-sphere. France, Italy, and Spain offer enough wines and wine stories to fill many chapters and indeed many books. And you will find them at your local library or favorite wine book retailer.

Have we covered every possibility? No, that would be impossible. Have we done enough to make the journey a success? You must be the judge of that.

THE ACCOUNTING

So now we must unpack our heavy case and list the contents. We certainly have a lot of wine, but I can see that there have been some problems. It seems that I have been very conservative in some places (just a few wines each from France and Italy, for example) and unexpectedly generous in others. The lack of consistency is a concern, but perhaps more alarming is this fact: we have not filled the case! In my attempt to always leave room for other discoveries further along the road, I have arrived here in London with only fifty-six wines in total. Around the world in eighty wines means eighty wines, not fifty-six. That is inexcusable. What can be done—set out on the road again?

No. Wait. I am forgetting where we are. There is no reason to go around the world again in search of these wines because we are here on the premises of England's (and maybe the world's) most famous wine shop. You can't find every wine in the world here, but you can find so many types of wines from so many places. Can we fill in the blank spots in our traveling case here? More selections from France or Italy? Wines from Hungary, Romania, Japan, Turkey, Greece, and Israel? Oh my, yes, and more beyond that. And, while it is hard to imagine a wine wonderland better than Berry Bros. & Rudd, it is a fact that parallel-universe wonderlands are an increasingly common feature of everyday life. It is no longer unusual for a shop or supermarket to carry hundreds or even thousands of different wines.

So, and you have been waiting for this, I invite you to fill in the remaining twenty-four spots on our list with your own selection of fantasy and favorite wines. You can even toss out some of my choices and substitute more of your own if you like, because our difference in taste, in wine, or in experiences, is something to be celebrated.

Were you frustrated in France, when I limited our selections to just a few red wines from Burgundy and Bordeaux? Then let yourself go a bit and add in your favorite wines from other regions and other styles. Here are a few to get you started.

Didier Dagueneau Silex, Pouilly-Fumé, Loire, France

Trimbach Riesling Cuvée Frédéric Émile, Alsace, France

Château de Beaucastel, Châteauneuf-du-Pape, Rhône, France

Terroir Feely Premier Or, Saussignac, Southwest, France

Château d'Yquem, Sauternes, Bordeaux, France

The Batali Impossibility Theorem means that it is impossible to somehow boil Italian wine down to its essence, because Italy and wine are both such complicated things. This is your chance to add in Italian wines of your dreams or your memories. Here are a few of mine inspired by our recent visits to Veneto and Friuli. The list could go on and on.

Rodaro Paolo Romain Refosco, Friuli Colli Orientali, Friuli–Venezia Giulia, Italy

Bastianich Calabrone, Friuli–Venezia Giulia, Italy

Valentina Cubi Morar, Amarone della Valpolicella Classico, Veneto, Italy

Maeli Estate Fior d'Arancio DOCG, Colli Euganei, Veneto, Italy

Cantina Produttori Cormòns Vino della Pace, Cormòns, Friuli–Venezia Giulia, Italy

With Château Musar as your inspiration, why not add more natural wines to the collection? Musar makes a white wine, for example, and an inexpensive red wine from younger vines. And then there are the natural wines from Georgia, if you can find them. Our favorites include Saperavi from Gotsa Wines and Pheasant's Tears and a lovely Rkatsiteli made by the monks at Alaverdi Monastery, where wine has been produced since 1011.

Then there's Spain. So many great wines. We must add a few more to the collection starting with Torres Mas La Plana, a rich single-vineyard Cabernet Sauvignon from the Penedès region. And how could I forget the Manzanos Wines Voché Selección Old Vines Graciano from Rioja? The list of beautiful Spanish wines goes on and on. Fill in your favorite here and don't forget to add some of the unforgettable whites from Rias Baixas, too.

How did we leave Spain without stocking up on sherry? I remember—we were caught up in my El Clásico soccer metaphor. No problem. The shop is filled with sherry wines and more are just around the corner. Here are a few to get you started. The Don Zoilo PX that I have put on the list was served at the end of a fantastic seafood meal at restaurant Madonnina del Pescatore in Senigallia, on the Italian Adriatic coast. Fantastic.

Tio Pepe Muy Seco Palomino Fino Sherry, Jerez, Spain

Osborne Very Old Rare Pedro Ximénez Viejo Sherry, Jerez, Spain

Gonzalez Byass Finest Dry Palo Cortado 1987 Vintage Sherry, Jerez, Spain

William & Humbert Don Zoilo Pedro Ximénez 12-year-old Sherry, Jerez, Spain

Portugal is a small country, as everyone will tell you if you visit, but it is big when it comes to wine. More port? Yes, please, and madeira, too. And some of the wonderful still wines must be represented as well. Here are a few to whet your appetite. Sue and I enjoyed the Graham's Tawny with Stilton cheese at the winery's fantastic restaurant looking out across the river to Porto. And we will never forget when the humble winegrowers of the Adega Cooperative Vidigueira serenaded us in Évora while we toasted them with their own wine at a banquet celebrating sustainable winemaking. Their traditional polyphonic singing was as memorable as the crisp white wine.

Graham's 20-Year-Old Tawny Port, Douro, Portugal

Quinta do Vesuvio DOC, Douro, Portugal

Broadbent 10-Year Malmsey, Madeira, Portugal

Adega Cooperative Vidigueira Vila dos Gamos DOC, Alentejo, Portugal

We made many friends and had wonderful experiences in South Africa. It is the wine country that is farthest away from our home in the United States, but the wines are close to our hearts. Here are some suggestions if you'd like to add a few more to our case.

Springfield Estate Méthode Ancienne Cabernet Sauvignon, Robertson, South Africa

Jordan Nine Yards Chardonnay, Stellenbosch, South Africa

Stark-Condé Three Pines Cabernet Sauvignon, Jonkershoek Valley, Stellenbosch, South Africa

Durbanville Hills Rhinofields Sauvignon Blanc, Durbanville Hills, South Africa

Paul Cluver Nine Flags Pinot Noir, Elgin, South Africa

Vilafonté Series M (or maybe Series C!), Stellenbosch, South Africa

Joubert-Tradauw Syrah, Tradouw Valley, South Africa

Our survey of New Latitude wines took us to Bali, Thailand, and India, but I don't think you will be surprised to learn that there are other tropical and semitropical regions that produce wines that are worth your attention. The Ulupalakua Syrah from Maui, Hawaii, is especially surprising. Hawaiian wine—must be made out of pineapples. And yes, there is pineapple wine made in Maui and it is better than you might guess. But there is also Syrah grown on a hillside near the sea and it will surprise you, too.

Vang Dalat Cardinal, Dalat, Vietnam

Ulupalakua Vineyards Syrah, Maui County, Hawaii

Salton Intenso Sparkling Brut, Serra Gaúcha, Brazil

Some of China's best wines are already included in our eighty-bottle case, but you might want to supplement them with other wines. If you want to go upscale, I recommend any of the wines from Grace Vineyards. But it is important to get an idea of the wines made by the largest producers, Changyu (stocked by Berry Bros. & Rudd) and Great Wall.

The Australian wine industry put together a long-term plan a few years ago that imagined a multistage approach to global wine market domination. Successful value wines were the first goal before moving upmarket. But the simple wines came to define Brand Australia and that next step has been a real challenge. There is a world of great wine in between Grange and Hill of Grace at the top and those supermarket wines on the bottom shelf. I challenge you to add your favorites to the list. Here are some suggestions.

Yalumba The Virgilius Viognier, Eden Valley, Australia

Seppeltsfield 100-year-old Para Vintage Tawny, Barossa Valley, Australia

Rockford Basket Press Shiraz, Barossa Valley, Australia

Hentley Farm The Stray Mongrel, Barossa Valley, Australia

Hahndorf Hill Winery Grüner Veltliner, Adelaide Hills, Australia

Jim Barry The Armagh Shiraz, Clare Valley, Australia

Yalumba The Signature Shiraz-Cabernet Sauvignon, Barossa Valley, Australia (Robert Hill Smith suggests the 1975 and the 1995 vintages)

Take this opportunity to add any cool-climate wines that you can find from England, Wales, or Tasmania (the Jansz sparkling wines may be the easiest to find in the United States). There are wines from many emerging cool-climate areas such as Nova Scotia in Canada, for example, and or Scandinavia. Wines are now produced in Norway, Sweden, and Denmark! Who knew?

There are many more wines waiting for you as you view the Southern Cross. Although you could simply add your favorite Sauvignon Blanc or Pinot Noir from New Zealand, Cabernet or Chardonnay from Chile, or Malbec from Argentina, I would encourage you to fill the case with other wines that do not so easily fit the stereotypes for these countries. I love the Rieslings from Framingham in New Zealand, for example, and those from the Bio Bio Valley in Chile. Bonarda from Argentina is worth seeking out as well as interesting red or white wine blends.

Do you have any room left? If so, you should add your favorite California wines here, both aristocratic like the Stag's Leap and democratic like Two-Buck Chuck. Sue and I are especially fond of the wines from Tres Sabores and Frog's Leap as well as Larkmead and Cain Five, but really there are hundreds of distinctive wines for you to enjoy.

More Riesling! There are so many great Riesling wines from all over the world, ranging from dry to sweet to very sweet. I hope you like Riesling as much as I do and can find room for a few of your favorite bottles! Trouble choosing? (Or maybe you haven't discovered the joys of Riesling yet?) Maybe you should book a flight to Seattle for the next Riesling Rendezvous in 2019!

Our Cannonball Run across North America revealed a continent filled to the brim with interesting wines and the stories to go with them. Here are a few for your consideration.

The Eyrie Vineyard Original Vines Pinot Noir, Dundee Hills, Oregon

Sandhill One Phantom Creek Vineyard, Okanagan Valley, Canada

Fielding Hills Winery Cabernet Franc, Wahluke Slope, Washington

Corliss Syrah, Columbia Valley, Washington

Reininger Winery Carmenère, Columbia Valley, Washington

Corvus Cellars SPS, Red Mountain, Washington

Hedges Family Estate Red Mountain, Red Mountain, Washington

Huston Vineyards Chicken Dinner Red, Snake River Valley, Idaho

Callaghan Winery Padres, Elgin, Arizona

Gruet Winery Grand Rosé, New Mexico

We traveled the world of wine on our adventure, but we couldn't stop everywhere, so if you have any room in your eighty-bottle case, fill the last few slots with these wines. Turkey has a long wine history, too. A white wine called Emir is worth seeking out, as well as almost any wine made from the hundreds of indigenous grape varieties. Uruguay and Peru make some nice wines, as you might expect given their Spanish colonial histories, and we did not have time to go to Austria and Hungary or Slovenia, Slovakia, Croatia, or the Czech Republic, either. Romania and Moldova? Next book—I promise! And Japan, too—the Koshu wine from Japan's Grace Winery is on my bucket list. Berry Bros. & Rudd is the perfect place to top up your case, but you don't have to go to London to experience a world of wine. So many wines, so little time. To paraphrase Johnson, a person who is tired of wine is tired of life. And you don't look tired to me!

VICTORY OR DEFEAT?

We have experienced a lot on this journey and hopefully learned a lot, too. Did we win or lose the challenge? To answer this I am going to appeal for one last time to Jules Verne's famous novel. Phileas Fogg won his bet, which is what we all remember best about the ending, but what you may not recall is that, after striving so hard for thousands of miles, he really didn't care about winning and losing because along the road he had found something else, something a lot more precious than any sum of money. He had found *happiness* and that was victory enough for him.

I said at the start that every wine tells a story and each wine in our eighty-bottle case must pull its weight in this regard. And I think we have succeeded. But then I said that there was a larger goal—that the stories taken together like a mosaic or Seurat painting must reveal a larger truth. But I didn't know what that truth was at the beginning. Now I do.

Wine's greater truth is its ability to make us happy. As happy as Phileas Fogg. This is a wonderful gift and especially precious because we do not necessarily need to circle the globe to find it!

And so it is for me because the journey has been so interesting and I am happy you came along for the ride (and that you made it through to the final page). Isn't it great the world is full of such interesting wines and people and stories. Victory or defeat? It is like the glass that is half empty or half full. My advice? Drink up that glass, however filled or not it might be, and pull another cork. Cheers!

Notes

CHAPTER 1: LONDON

1. Facts about the Reform Club are taken from the club's website, which can be found at http://www.reformclub.com (accessed July 29, 2014).

2. "During the Middle Ages, wine was relatively cheap and plentiful in Britain," the *Oxford Companion to Wine* reports. "Wines from Germany, Portugal, Spain, Italy, Greece, the Mediterranean islands, and the Holy Land could all be found in London taverns, as well as those from France." Jancis Robinson, editor, *Oxford Companion to Wine,* 3rd ed. (New York: Oxford University Press, 2006). This quote is taken from the article on "British Influence on Wine," which can be found online at http://www.jancisrobinson.com/ocw/detail/british-influence-on-the-wine-trade (accessed July 30, 2015).

3. Jules Verne, *Around the World in Eighty Days* (New York: Sterling, 2008).

4. I told the story of how modern London became the "center of the earth" for wine trade, auctions, and media in my book *Wine Wars* (Lanham, MD: Rowman & Littlefield, 2011). Berry Bros. & Rudd was featured in that book, too, along with the Tesco supermarket chain, which was then the world's largest retailer of wine.

5. Michael Palin's series is available on DVD, as described here: http://www.imdb.com/title/tt0096536 (accessed July 31, 2015). Palin wrote a book about the filming that makes very good reading. Michael Palin, *Around the World in 80 Days* (London: BBC Books, 1989).

CHAPTER 2: FRANCE

1. This chapter is inspired by Jean-Robert Pitte's brilliant book *Bordeaux/ Burgundy: A Vintage Rivalry,* English translation by M.B. DeBoise (Berkeley: University of California Press, 2008). The cover of the book features the two types of bottles.

2. Jancis Robinson MW noted the physical sensations of Burgundy and Bordeaux in her BBC television series *Jancis Robinson's Wine Course.*

3. I wrote about these big bag, big box wines in my 2015 book, *Money, Taste, and Wine: It's Complicated!* (Lanham, MD: Rowman & Littlefield, 2015).

4. Pitte, *Burgundy/Bordeaux,* pp. 41–42.

5. I wrote about Bordeaux's distinctive money madness, the annual *en primeur* pre-sale campaign, in *Money, Taste, and Wine: It's Complicated!*

6. Richard Woodard, "Henry Jayer Tops DRC as World's Most Expensive Wine," *Decanter* online (August 10, 2015), http://www.decanter.com/wine-news/henri-jayer-tops-drc-as-worlds-most-expensive-wine-270029 (accessed August 10, 2015).

7. Elaine Sciolino, "A Sweet Victory for Burgundy," *New York Times* (August 20, 2015), p. D7.

8. Wine-searcher.com reports an average price of $1,964 per standard bottle for that 1994 Petrus, so it is hard to imagine what a double magnum of it might cost! The Amoureuses Burgundy is a bargain by comparison with an average price of nearly four hundred dollars. The reputations of these regions are rooted in the quality and scarcity of their finest wines.

9. Mike Veseth, *Extreme Wine* (Lanham, MD: Rowman & Littlefield, 2013), pp. 50–51.

10. Burgundy wines are made with conventional fermentation, often using whole clusters of grapes, while Beaujolais features the use of carbonic maceration, where the whole grapes are fermented in an anaerobic environment so that initial fermentation take place within the grapes themselves!

CHAPTER 3: ITALY

1. Parts of this chapter are adapted from a talk I gave at Vino 2015, a conference sponsored by the Italian Trade Commission and held in New York City in February

2015. Thanks to the Italian Trade Commission for their support. My fellow economics geeks will appreciate that the title of this chapter is inspired by Arrow's Impossibility Theorem, one of the most important results in twentieth-century welfare economics theory.

2. Ian D'Agata, *Native Wine Grapes of Italy* (Berkeley: University of California Press, 2014).

3. Jancis Robinson, Julia Harding, and José Vouillamoz, *Wine Grapes* (New York: HarperCollins Ecco, 2012).

4. Gianni Fabrizio, Eleonora Guerini, and Marco Sabellico (editors), *Italian Wines 2015* (New York: Gambero Rosso, 2014).

5. Mike Veseth, *Money, Taste, and Wine: It's Complicated!* (Lanham, MD: Rowman & Littlefield, 2015).

6. Andrea Seger and Gerald B. White, "Marketing Italian Wine in the U.S. Market: A Case Study of Cantine Riunite," in A. Kiadoó (editor), *Vine and Wine Economy* (Amsterdam: Elsevier, 2012).

7. Like many wines, Lambrusco can be simple or sophisticated; Cantina Della Volta makes some that receive the *Tre Bicchieri* award each year.

8. George Taber, *To Cork or Not to Cork* (New York: Scribner's, 2007).

9. Michael Veseth, *Mountains of Debt* (New York: Oxford University Press, 1990).

CHAPTER 4: SYRIA, LEBANON, AND GEORGIA

1. Randall Heskett and Joel Butler, *Divine Vintage: Following the Wine Trail from Genesis to the Modern Age* (New York: Palgrave Macmillan, 2012).

2. Mike Veseth, *Wine Wars* (Lanham, MD: Rowman & Littlefield, 2011).

3. Don and Petie Kladstrup, *Wine and War: The French, the Nazis, and the Battle for France's Greatest Treasure* (New York: Broadway Books, 2001).

4. References used in this section include Andreane Williams, "Squeezing Grapes under Syrian War Clouds," *Al Jazeera* (June 7, 2014); Henry Samuel, "Syrian Vineyard Making the World's Most Dangerous Wine," *The Telegraph* (June 28, 2015) and Suzanne Mustacich, "Wines of War," *Wine Spectator* (November 11, 2014).

5. Heskett and Butler, *Divine Vintage*, p. 160.

6. Heskett and Butler, *Divine Vintage*, p. 155. I wrote about the cultural elements of French colonial rule in my 2005 book *Globaloney*.

7. Sources for this part of the chapter include Jamie Goode and Sam Harrop, *Authentic Wine: Toward Natural and Sustainable Winemaking* (Berkeley: University of California Press, 2011); Alice Feiring, "The Iconic Wine List (Natural Style)," *The Feiring Line* (May 22, 2013) and "So Château Musar Is Natural," *Wine, Naturally* (November 23, 2010). Many tributes to Serge Hochar after his death mention his contribution to the natural wine movement.

8. Look for a fuller account of what we learned about wine wars in Georgia in my next book.

9. For an interesting introduction to this wine region see *Uncorking the Caucasus: Wines from Turkey, Armenia, and Georgia* by Matt Horkey and Charine Tan (Exotic Wine Travel, 2016).

10. Special thanks to Bartholomew Broadbent for telling me the full story of that 1984 wine.

CHAPTER 5: SPAIN

1. An excellent discussion of the history of the Algerian wine industry can be found in Giulio Meloni and Johan Swinnen, "The Rise and Fall of the World's Largest Wine Exporter—And Its Institutional Legacy." *Journal of Wine Economics* 9:1 (2014), pp. 3–33. Rod Phillips also discusses Algeria's rise and fall in *French Wine: A History* (Berkeley: University of California Press, 2016).

2. Meloni and Swinnen, "Rise and Fall," p. 11.

3. Meloni and Swinnen argue that the appellation regulations are the true legacy of the Algerian wine industry in today's world.

4. John and Erica Platter, *Africa Uncorked: Travels in Extreme Wine Territory* (South San Francisco: Wine Appreciation Guild, 2002), pp. 33–35.

5. I discussed how football became association football and then soccer in my 2005 book *Globaloney*.

6. Data reported here are from the entry "Rioja" in the *Oxford Companion to Wine, 4th ed.*, edited by Jancis Robinson and Julia Harding (New York: Oxford University Press, 2015), pp. 614–616.

7. See "Vega Sicilia, a Ribera del Duero Legend" by Luis Gutiérrez at JancisRobinson.com (January 30, 2012), http://www.jancisrobinson.com/articles/vega-sicilia-a-ribera-del-duero-legend (accessed September 24, 2015).

8. Gutiérrez, "Vega Sicilia, a Ribera del Duero Legend."

9. The Italian method is also called the Charmat bulk process for making sparkling wines.

CHAPTER 6: PORTUGAL

1. This section draws from the article on port in the *Oxford Companion to Wine,* 3rd ed., edited by Jancis Robinson (New York: Oxford University Press, 2006).

2. Martin Page, *The First Global Village: How Portugal Changed the World* (Alfragide, Portugal: Casa das Letras, 2002).

3. David Hancock, *Oceans of Wine: Madeira and the Emergence of American Trade and Taste* (New Haven, CT: Yale University Press, 2009). A distinguished historian, Hancock got interested when his planned sunny vacation to Funchal was rained out. With nothing much to do, he visited the madeira lodges and discovered a fascinating topic for a book.

4. I wrote about this wine, which I have tasted twice, in my 2013 book *Extreme Wine.*

CHAPTER 7: OUT OF AFRICA

1. I wrote about Lanzarote in the first chapter of my 2013 book *Extreme Wine* and I just can't resist including it here, too. This section is adapted from that source.

2. For a fuller description see Jacques Fanet (translated from the French by Florence Brutton), *Great Wine Terroirs* (Berkeley: University of California Press, 2004), pp. 226–27.

3. Special thanks to Gwen and Phil Phibbs for their Lanzarote wine fieldwork.

4. *Africa Uncorked: Travels in Extreme Wine Territory* by John and Erica Platter (San Francisco: The Wine Appreciation Guild, 2002).

5. Louise Leakey's winery blog can be found at http://www.zabibu.org (accessed November 23, 2015).

6. The *Financial Times* ran a story in its November 20, 2015, edition about the luxury tourism side of the project (http://www.ft.com/intl/cms/s/0/e56aeb9c-8f06-11e5-8be4-3506bf20cc2b.html#slide0, accessed November 23, 2015). By the numbers: five-day tour from $14,188 per person, including a $3750 donation to the Turkana Basin Institute.

7. Clive Cookson, "Lunch with the FT: Richard Leakey," *Financial Times* (December 5, 2015), http://www.ft.com/intl/cms/s/0/1ecd7040-99b0-11e5-9228-87e603d47bdc.html (accessed December 5, 2015).

8. Tim James, *Wines of the New South Africa: Tradition and Revolution* (Berkeley: University of California Press, 2013), p. 23. James's book is a great source for anyone wanting to learn more about South African wine today.

9. Governor Stell's name adorns the city of Stellenbosch, an important university and wine center.

10. You can read more about this experience in the final chapter of my 2013 book *Extreme Wine.*

11. If I had taken a different route that day, I might have passed through another township where grapes are grown and wine is made! BBC News reports small-scale production at Township Winery in Nyanga-East near Cape Town. See Pumza Fihlani, "Wine Grown in a South African Township," *BBC News* (December 10, 2015), http://www.bbc.com/news/world-africa-34592529 (accessed December 10, 2015).

12. The South African wine industry obviously cannot solve the nation's problems, but as I wrote in the final chapter of *Extreme Wine,* many wineries are doing what they can to improve current conditions and future prospects for their workers and communities.

13. Joubert told us that one of his secret advantages in making the Rupert & Rothschild Chardonnay was access to wonderful grapes from his family's Barrydale farm.

14. The discussion of Four Cousins is based on correspondence with Phillip Retief and Mary-Lyn Foxcroft's Cape Wine master's thesis, "Growing the Consumption of Wine amongst Emerging Market Consumers in South Africa" (January 2009). Foxcroft's thesis is available at http://www.capewineacademy.co.za/dissertations/capewinemaster_foxcroft_growing_wine_consumption.pdf (accessed November 27, 2015).

15. Foxworth reports that concentrated juice is added to some of the wines to soften them and lower the alcohol content.

16. The 2014 *Platter's Guide* describes the Four Cousins Dry Red as "charmingly rustic," perfect for a braai (South Africa's distinctive and wildly popular type of barbecue feast). The sparkling Sauvignon Blanc was singled out for special praise.

CHAPTER 8: INDIA AND BEYOND

1. Jancis Robinson, "New Latitude Wines" (May 31, 2004), http://www.jancisrobinson.com/articles/new-latitude-wines (accessed December 21, 2015).

2. Parts of this section are adapted from my 2013 book *Extreme Wine* and from "Sababay Wines of Bali: New Latitudes, New Flavors, New Frontiers" by Ali Hoover, which was published on WineEconomist.com on August 26, 2014, http://wineeconomist.com/2014/08/26/sababay (accessed December 21, 2015).

3. Okay, well I guess I did know this, since wine's social change power was a theme of the final chapter of my 2015 book *Money, Taste, and Wine: It's Complicated!*

4. "Malaga Blanc" in Jancis Robinson, Julia Harding, and José Vouillamoz, *Wine Grapes* (New York: Ecco/HarperCollins, 2012), p. 568.

5. Some parts of this section are adapted and revised from my 2013 book *Extreme Wine*.

6. Two excellent profiles of Sula and Rajeev Samant are Erica Berenstein, "Turning India on to Wine" *Wine-Searcher.com* (October 29, 2012), http://www.wine-searcher.com/m/2012/10/sula-vineyards-turning-india-on-to-wine (accessed December 26, 2015) and Marguerite Rigoglioso, "The Mondavi of Mumbai," *Stanford Magazine* (January/February 2004), https://alumni.stanford.edu/get/page/magazine/article/?article_id=36274 (accessed December 26. 2015).

7. In fact, the Thompson Seedless grapes are a variety with three uses—fresh table grapes, dried as raisins, or crushed to make perfectly drinkable if not sophisticated table wine.

8. Anand Narasimhan and Aparna M. Dogra, "Case Study: Developing Indians' Taste for Wine," *Financial Times* (December 5, 2011), http://www.ft.com/intl/cms/s/0/477c27f0-04ab-11e1-91d9-00144feabdc0.html#axzz3vTGApGdu (accessed December 26, 2015).

CHAPTER 9: SHANGRI-LA

1. James Hilton, *Lost Horizon* (New York: William Morrow, 1933). By the way, the reference to the Maharajah of Chandrapore is very clever. Chandrapore is a fictional location in E.M. Forster's novel *A Passage to India*.

2. Key resources I used in this section are *Thirsty Dragon: China's Lust for Bordeaux and the Threat to the World's Best Wines* by Suzanne Mustacich (New York: Henry Holt, 2015), "The Vineyards of Shangri-La" by Jane Anson in *Decanter* (September 2015) pp. 28–33, and "Winemaking in Shangri-La" by Jim Boyce in the February 2016 issue of *Meininger's Wine Business International*, pp. 38–40.

3. By formal agreement at the time of the merger, the company is always spelled-out as Möet Hennessy Louis Vuitton and always abbreviated as LVMH. Go figure.

4. David Roach and Warwick Ross, *Red Obsession* (Lion Rock Films, 2013).

5. That honor might go to Wuha, about one hundred miles away in Inner Mongolia on the edge of the Gobi Desert, where a winery called Château Hansen makes award-winning wines. See Andrew Rose, "Chateau Hansen: Welcome to the Gobi Desert," *Decanter.com* (May 1, 2014), http://www.decanter.com/features/chateau-hansen-welcome-to-the-gobi-desert-245923 (accessed January 8, 2016).

6. Jancis Robinson visited Ningxia in 2012. Her informative reports can be found on her subscription website *JancisRobinson.com*, http://www.jancisrobinson.com/articles/chinas-most-promising-wine-province (accessed January 8, 2016).

7. My personal experience with Changyu wine differs somewhat from Sun Yat-sen's. As I wrote in *Wine Wars*, my first taste of Changyu or Chinese wines of any sort happened a few years ago when Brian West brought me a bottle of the 1999 Changyu Cabernet Sauvignon when he returned from a semester in Beijing. I sampled it at a party that some of my wine students threw to celebrate the end of the semester and the Changyu was the star of the evening because of its peculiar character. The aroma, according to a tasting note I found on the Internet, was ashtray, coffee grounds, and urinal crust. It really was! There were good reasons for variable wine quality, I wrote, because the supply chain was so fragmented and consumer expectations low. Plus there was the location itself, where climate and proximity to the Yellow Sea meant high humidity and vulnerability to mold and fungal diseases.

8. See "Möet's Chinese Wine 'A Logistical Nightmare'" by Patrick Schmidt, *The Drinks Business* (June 2016), available on the web at www.thedrinksbusiness.com/2016/060moets-chinese-wine-a-logistical-nightmare (accessed June 8, 2016).

CHAPTER 10: AUSTRALIA

1. The basic outline of the history of Penfolds and Grange can be found on the company website: https://www.penfolds.com/en-us/heritage-and-winemaking/the-story-of-grange (accessed March 4, 2016). I was especially impressed by the video that was produced to tell the wine's story, featuring a bespoke score and narration by Russell Crowe!

2. Port must come from Portugal today and sherries from Spain, according to contemporary wine-naming rules, although some practices were "grandfathered in." Thus one of the few American sparkling wines that can call themselves Champagne is also one of the least expensive: Cook's California Champagne.

3. We were able to taste such wines from 1949, 1921, and 1913 during our visit to the historic Seppeltsfield winery and they were impressive.

4. Robert Geddes, *Australian Wine Vintages 2014* (Australia: Geddes A Drink Publications, 2013), p. 48.

5. My discussion of Henschke and Hill of Grace draws from Graeme Lofts, *Heart & Soul: Australia's First Families of Wine* (Melbourne: John Wiley & Sons Australia, 2010).

6. I wrote in *Extreme Wine* about Australia's history of wine boom and bust.

7. This section is adapted from several columns that appeared on *The Wine Economist* in 2015.

8. I have heard it said that it is "shirtsleeves to shirtsleeves in three generations" here in the U.S. and it amounts to the same thing.

9. "Impact Seminar Snapshot: Treasury Wine's Clarke on the Globalization of Winemaking," *Shanken News Daily*, March 25, 2015, http://www.shankennewsdaily.com/index.php/2015/03/25/12004/impact-seminar-snapshot-treasury-wines-clarke-on-the-globalization-of-wine-marketing (accessed March 7, 2016).

10. The history of Southcorp is based on analysis at FundingUniverse.com, http://www.fundinguniverse.com/company-histories/southcorp-limited-history (accessed March 6, 2016).

CHAPTER 11: TASMANIA

1. We stayed with growers in the Barossa Valley, too—Blickenstall Barossa Valley Retreat on Rifle Range Road in Tanunda.

2. Stephen Brook, "Best Pinot Noir Wines Outside of Burgundy," *Decanter.com*, http://www.decanter.com/wine-reviews-tastings/best-pinot-noir-wines-outside-burgundy-296918 (accessed April 4, 2016).

3. Robert Hill Smith of Yalumba and Janz and Michael Hill Smith of Shaw+Smith and Tolpuddle are brothers.

4. Neil Beckett (editor), *1001 Wines You Must Taste Before You Die* (New York: Universe Publishing, 2008).

5. See Gregory V. Jones, "Climate, Grapes and Wine: Structure and Suitability in a Changing Climate," *Proceedings of the XXVIIIth Congress on Viticulture & Climate* 2012, pp. 19–28.

6. Data from NASA and NOAA research. See https://www.nasa.gov/press-release/nasa-noaa-data-show-2016-warmest-year-on-record-globally (accessed March 10, 2017).

7. Jancis Robinson, "English Sparkling Wine," *Financial Times* (March 3, 2016), http://www.ft.com/intl/cms/s/2/cd022df2-e0c5-11e5-8d9b-e88a2a889797.html (accessed April 4, 2016).

8. A. Nesbit et al., "Impact of Recent Climate Change and Weather Variability on the Viability of UK Viticulture—Combining Weather and Climate Records with UK Producers' Perspectives." *Australian Journal of Grape and Wine Research* (2016), pp. 1–12.

9. "Tasmania Charts a New Course: Water into Wine." *The Economist* (February 13, 2016), http://www.economist.com/news/asia/21692945-island-state-bets-water-revive-its-fortunes-water-wine (accessed April 5, 2016).

CHAPTER 12: SOUTHERN CROSS

1. "Southern Cross" was written by Stephen Stills and Rick and Michael Curtis.

2. I wrote about New Zealand's wine history in Chapter 4 of my 2011 book *Wine Wars*. Sue and I visited the Kerikeri site and saw old etchings of the landscape that clearly showed the vineyard.

3. World wine production data for 2015 compiled from OIV data. See http://www.oiv.int/public/medias/2256/en-communique-de-presse-octobre-2015.pdf (accessed April 8, 2016).

4. Chile re-emerged into the world market with the same reputation that it had in the past. Great value wine. This is both a blessing and a curse because it is better to be known as good value than bad value, but I think the Chilean producers would like to be known for their finest wines as well as their relatively low prices. This is one area where New Zealand had an advantage over Chile. New Zealand wines were essentially unknown in world markets before they made their entrance in the 1970s at a premium price. Chilean wines were stuck with an existing label. The wines themselves have improved and become more interesting year after year as the many diverse local *terroirs* are investigated.

5. You can read the press release announcing the world's most powerful wine brand at http://www.prnewswire.com/news-releases/concha-y-toro-retains-leadership-as-worlds-most-powerful-wine-brand-300107575.html (accessed April 8, 2016).

6. The rise is chronicled in a film called *Boom Varietal: The Rise of Argentina Malbec*, directed by Sky Pinnick, 2011.

7. See *Vino Argentino: An Insider's Guide to the Wines and Wine Country of Argentina* by Laura Catena (Chronicle Books, 2010) and Ian Mount, *The Vineyard at the End of the World: Maverick Winemakers and the Rebirth of Malbec* (New York: Norton, 2011)

CHAPTER 13: NAPA VALLEY WINE TRAIN

1. This history is taken from Cynthia Sweeney, "Napa Valley Wine Train Adds New Train, Tour" *North Bay Business Journal* (May 23, 2016), http://www.northbaybusinessjournal.com/northbay/napacounty/5626654-181/napa-valley-wine-train-quattro-tour (accessed May 23, 2016).

2. Current tours and prices can be found at the Napa Valley Wine Train's website at http://winetrain.com (accessed May 23, 2016).

3. Destination Analysis, Inc., *Napa Valley Visitor Industry: 2014 Economic Impact Report.* Visit Napa Valley, 2015. Available online at http://sodacanyonroad.org/docs/Napa%20Valley%202014%20Economic%20Impact%20Report.pdf (accessed May 23, 2016).

4. See the Napa Vision 2050 website for background and current news, http://napavision2050.org/about.php (accessed June 21, 2016).

5. Paul Franson, "Top Local Wine Stories of 2015," *Napa Valley Register* (December 31, 2015), http://napavalleyregister.com/lifestyles/food-and-cooking/wine/

columnists/paul-franson/top-local-wine-stories-of/article_ac35abd0-8ed4-510c-a8c9-5a6cfef1663d.html (accessed May 24, 2015).

6. Paul Franson, "Two Billion-Buck Chuck," *Wines & Vines* (January 26, 2016), http://www.winesandvines.com/template.cfm?section=news&content=163823 (accessed May 24, 2016).

7. Richard G. Peterson, *The Winemaker* (Meadowlark Publishing: 2015), pp. 359–61.

8. This winery also has a personal meaning for me—it's the place where my career as a wine economist began. I wrote about it (without naming names) in the first chapter of *Wine Wars*.

CHAPTER 14: A RIESLING RENDEZVOUS

1. I wrote about IPNC in the chapter on "Extreme Wine People" of my 2013 book *Extreme Wine*. Check out that book for further information. I was on the faculty of the "University of Pinot" and the chapter gives a sense of that experience.

2. You can get a sense of Terry Theise and his intense personality by reading his book *Reading Between the Wines* (Berkeley: University of California Press, 2010).

3. Jamie Goode is a former science editor who now writes about wine with a distinct scientific way of looking at things. His discussion of the limitations of analytical data in understanding Riesling taste can be found on his blog at http://www.wineanorak.com/wineblog/wine-science/riesling-rendezvous-why-analytical-data-dont-tell-us-much-about-the-taste-of-riesling (accessed July 25, 2016).

4. See John Winthrop Haeger, *Riesling Rediscovered: Bold, Bright, and Dry* (Berkeley: University of California Press, 2016).

5. Stuart Pigott, *Best White Wine on Earth: The Riesling Story* (New York: Abrams, 2014).

6. See Jancis Robinson, "Kabinett Under Threat," JancisRobinson.com (June 10, 2008), http://www.jancisrobinson.com/articles/kabinett-under-threat (accessed May 27, 2016).

7. See my 2005 book, *Globaloney* (Rowman & Littlefield) for my analysis of globalization stories.

CHAPTER 15: CANNONBALL RUN

1. The event is named for Erwin George "Cannon Ball" Baker, who blazed the route in 1933. His Graham-Paige model 57 Blue Streak 8 car completed the course in fifty-three hours and thirty minutes.

2. For the record, Google Maps seems to think that you can drive from New York to Los Angeles via Interstate 80 in about forty-one hours (if you make all the lights). Good luck!

3. Paul Franson, "Number of U.S. Wineries Reaches 8,702," *Wine Business Monthly* (February 2016), pp. 76–77.

4. Winemaking in Canada is concentrated in Ontario and British Columbia. Mississippi has the fewest wineries with only three. Alaska has five and Hawaii four.

5. Jancis Robinson and Linda Murphy, *American Wine: The Ultimate Companion to the Wines and Wineries of the United States* (Berkeley: University of California Press, 2013).

6. The L'Ecole 41 winery is located in Lowden, Washington, which used to be called Frenchtown because of its link to those French-Canadian trappers.

7. See Thomas Pinney, *The Makers of American Wine* (Berkeley: University of California Press, 2012). Chapter 2 is titled "Nicholas Longworth: The Necessary Entrepreneur."

8. My friends at the American Association of Wine Economists organized a "Judgment of Princeton" tasting of French versus New Jersey wines when they met in that state a few years ago. New Jersey won. Now you know.

9. I wrote about Boordy Vineyards in *Wine Wars*.

10. Robinson and Murphy, *American Wine*, p. 7.

The Wine List

WINES OF THE PEOPLE

- Mouton Cadet Rouge, Bordeaux, France
- Georges Duboeuf Beaujolais Nouveau, Beaujolais, France
- Riunite Lambrusco, Emilia-Romagna, Italy
- Cuvée du Président, Algeria
- Mateus Rosé, Portugal
- Four Cousins Sweet Rosé, South Africa
- Charles Shaw Chardonnay, California
- Tio Pepe Muy Seco Palomino Fino Sherry, Jerez, Spain

NOBLE WINES

- Chateau Petrus, Bordeaux, France
- Marchesi Antinori Chianti Classico Riserva DOCG, Tuscany, Italy
- Château Musar Red, Bekaa Valley, Lebanon
- Vega Sicilia Único, Ribera del Duero, Spain
- Sandeman Vintage Port, Douro, Portugal
- Kanonkop Black Label Pinotage, Stellenbosch, South Africa
- Penfolds Grange Bin 95 Shiraz, South Australia, Australia
- Henschke Hill of Grace Shiraz, Eden Valley, Australia
- Domaine A Cabernet Sauvignon, Coal River, Tasmania, Australia
- Nicolás Catena Zapata Cabernet Sauvignon–Malbec, Mendoza, Argentina

- Jordan Nine Yards Chardonnay, Stellenbosch, South Africa
- Vilafonte Series M, Stellenbosch, South Africa
- Stark-Condé Three Pines Cabernet Sauvignon, Jonkershoek Valley, Stellenbosch, South Africa
- Paul Cluver Nine Flags Pinot Noir, Elgin, South Africa
- Yalumba The Virgilius Viognier, Eden Valley, Australia
- Yalumba The Signature Shiraz-Cabernet Sauvignon, Barossa Valley, Australia
- Rockford Basket Press Shiraz, Barossa Valley, Australia
- Jim Barry The Armagh Shiraz, Clare Valley, Australia
- Stag's Leap Wine Cellars Cabernet Sauvignon, Napa Valley, California
- The Eyrie Vineyards Original Vines Pinot Noir, Dundee Hills, Oregon
- Corliss Syrah, Columbia Valley, Washington

WINES THAT WARM THE SOUL

- Taylor Fladgate LBV Port, Douro, Portugal
- Terroir Feely Premier Or, Saussignac, Southwest, France
- Chateau d'Yquem, Sauternes, Bordeaux, France
- Osborne Very Old Rare Pedro Ximénez Viejo Sherry, Jerez, Spain
- William & Humbert Don Zoilo Pedro Ximenez 12-year-old Sherry, Jerez, Spain
- Graham's 20-year-old Tawny Port, Douro, Portugal

WINES FOR PHILOSOPHERS

- Seppeltsfield 100-year-old Para Vintage Tawny, Barossa Valley, Australia
- 1875 Barbeito Malvasia, Madeira, Portugal
- Venissa Venezia, Isola di Mazzorbo, Veneto, Italy
- Rodaro Paolo Romain Refosco, Friuli Colli Orientali, Friuli–Venezia Giulia, Italy
- Silver Heights Family Reserve, China
- Tolpuddle Pinot Noir, Coal River, Tasmania, Australia
- Pewsey Vales The Contours Riesling, Eden Valley, Australia
- Tantalus Old Vines Riesling, Okanagan Valley, British Columbia, Canada
- Gonzalez Byass Finest Dry Palo Cortado 1987 Vintage Sherry, Jerez, Spain
- Mendel Wines Semillon, Mendoza, Argentina

- Robert Mondavi To Kalon Fumé Blanc, Napa Valley, California
- L'Ecole 41 Ferguson Vineyard, Walla Walla, Washington
- Barboursville Vineyards Octagon, Virginia
- Didier Dagueneau Silex, Pouilly-Fumé, Loire, France
- Trimbach Riesling Cuvée Frédéric Émile, Alsace, France
- Château de Beaucastel, Châteauneuf-du-Pape, Rhône, France
- Springfield Estate Méthode Ancienne Cabernet Sauvignon, Robertson, South Africa

WINES FOR ROMANTICS

- Maison Joseph Drouhin Chambolle-Musigny Amoreuses, Burgundy, France
- Maeli Estate Fior d'Arancio DOCG, Colli Euganei, Veneto, Italy
- Broadbent 10-Year Malmsey, Madeira, Portugal
- 2015 Rupert & Rothschild Baroness Nadine Chardonnay, Western Cape, South Africa
- Barboursville Vineyards Nebbiolo Reserve, Virginia
- Bastianich Calabrone, Friuli–Venezia Giulia, Italy
- Valentina Cubi Morar, Amarone della Valpolicella Classico, Veneto, Italy
- Cantina Produttori Cormons Vino della Pace, Cormòns, Friuli–Venezia Giulia, Italy
- Quinta do Vesuvio DOC, Douro, Portugal
- Adega Cooperative Vidigueira Vila dos Gamos DOC, Alentejo, Portugal
- Bacalhoa Moscatel du Setúbal, Setúbal, Portugal
- Torres Mas La Plana, Penedès, Spain
- Manzanos Wines Voché Selección Old Vines Graciano, Rioja, Spain
- Klein Constantia Vin de Constance, Constantia, South Africa
- Weingut Dönnhoff Niederhäuser Hermannshöle Auslese, Nahe Valley, Germany
- Reininger Winery Carmenère, Columbia Valley, Washington
- Corvus Cellars SPS, Red Mountain, Washington
- Hedges Family Estate Red Mountain, Red Mountain, Washington
- Dr. Loosen and Chateau Ste. Michelle Eroica Riesling, Columbia Valley, Washington
- Fielding Hills Winery Cabernet Franc, Wahluke Slope, Washington
- R&G Rolland Galarreta, Rioja, Spain

- Brancott Estate Sauvignon Blanc, Marlborough, New Zealand
- Concha y Toro Casillero del Diablo Carmenère, Chile

WINES FOR ADVENTURERS

- Domaine de Bargylus Red, Syria
- Colomé Auténico Malbec, Salta, Argentina
- Sababay Moscato d'Bali, Indonesia
- Monsoon Valley Malaga Blanc/Colombard, Thailand
- Sula Dindori Reserve Shiraz, Nashik, India, and Sula Sauvignon Blanc, Nashik, India
- Grace Vineyard Tasya's Reserve Marselan 2012, China
- Durbanville Hills Rhinofields Sauvignon Blanc, Durbanville Hills, South Africa
- Joubert-Tradauw Syrah, Tradouw Valley, South Africa
- Vang Dalat Cardinal, Dalat, Vietnam
- Ulupalakua Vineyards Syrah, Maui County, Hawaii
- Hentley Farm The Stray Mongrel, Barossa Valley, Australia
- Hahndorf Hill Winery Grüner Veltliner, Adelaide Hills, Australia
- Grace Vineyards Koshu, Japan
- Sandhill One Phantom Creek Vineyard, Okanagan Valley, British Columbia, Canada
- Huston Vineyards Chicken Dinner Red, Snake River Valley, Idaho
- Callaghan Winery Padres, Elgin, Arizona
- Shangri-La Winery Ao Yun, China
- Helan Qing Xue's Jiabeilan Cabernet blend, China
- Quartz Reef Pinot Noir, Central Otago, New Zealand
- Iago's Wine Chardakhi, Chinuri, Republic of Georgia
- Pheasant's Tears Shavkapito, Kartli, Republic of Georgia
- Gotsa Family Wines Saperavi, Republic of Georgia
- Alaverdi Monastery Marani Rkatsiteli, Republic of Georgia

CELEBRATION WINES

- Champagne Pol Roger Cuvée Winston Churchill, Champagne, France
- Carpenè Malvolti Conegliano Valdobbiadene Prosecco Superiore, Veneto, Italy

- Silvano Follador Valdobbiadene Prosecco Superiore di Cartizze Brut Nature, Veneto, Italy
- Gran Codorníu Gran Reserva, Catalonia, Spain
- Freixenet Cordon Negro, Catalonia, Spain
- Domaine Chandon (Ningxia) Brut Rosé, China
- Nyetimber Classic Cuvée, Sussex, England
- Salton Intenso Sparkling Brut, Serra Gaúcha, Brazil
- Gruet Winery Grand Rosé, New Mexico

Acknowledgments

I owe many people a debt of gratitude for the support, knowledge, and constructive criticism they have given freely to me as I researched and then wrote (and rewrote and re-rewrote) this book. Here is a shout-out to some of them who share credit for anything good you may find in these pages but are blameless of any errors or outrages I may have perpetrated herein.

Thanks first of all to my readers, both those who have read and responded to my earlier books and readers of the Wine Economist blog. I can't overstate how many good ideas my readers have provided and how many bad ideas they have shot down. Special thanks to Ken Bernsohn for his brilliant insights and constructive criticism. Then I need to thank all the wine industry groups that have invited me to speak across the United States and around the world, letting me get to know new wine people, visit new wine regions, and taste wonderful wines. Thanks as well to my audiences, who have been patient and supportive as I have worked out my ideas in front of them.

I owe huge debt to my global network of wine industry experts and my "Proctor Street Irregulars" research assistants who give so freely of their time to answer my queries and suggest the real questions that I ought to be asking. I am also grateful to the University of Puget Sound for giving me the opportunity to teach and write about the world of wine.

Here are some special people who deserve special thanks starting with Allan, Holden, and PJ Sapp (for sharing their big bottle of Château Petrus with us), Lowell and Dorothy Daun, Ron and Mary Thomas, Phil and Gwen Phibbs, Ken and Rosemary Willman, Randy Miller, Richard Pichler and Bonny Main, Michael and Nancy Morrell.

Thanks to Professor Luigi Galletto and everyone we met at the Scuola Enologica di Conegliano, Matteo Bilson at Venissa, and Vincenza Kelly and the New York staff of the Italian Trade Commission. Extreme thanks to Bartholomew Broadbent and Marc Hochar, George Piradashvili, Beka Gotsadze, Iago Bitarishvili, John H. Wurdeman V, and kind regards to Javier Ruiz de Galaretta. *Obrigado* (that's Portuguese for thank you) to George Sandeman, Luís Sottomayor, Paul Symington, António Filipe, Antonio Amorim, Carlos de Jesus, Fernando Geddes, and Edouardo Medeiro.

A salute to all our South African friends including Paul Cluver and his father Dr. Paul Cluver, Carina Gous, Martin Moore and Albert Gerber, Cobus, Meyer and Schalk-Willem Joubert, Danie De Wet, Rico Basson, Johan Krige; Kathy and Gary Jordan, Dalene Steyn, Norma and Mike Ratcliffe, and Phillip Retief.

The list goes on: Rajeev Samant, Evy Gozaly, Ali Hoover, Mariam Anderson, Judy Chan, Edouard Cointreau, Pierre Ly, Cynthia Howson, Suzanne Mustacich, Jane Anson, Jean-Guillaume Prats, Brian West. More thank yous to Kym Anderson, Diana Phibbs, Robert Hill Smith, Stephen and Pru Henschke, John Duval, Tom Barry, Robert Geddes, Peter Althaus, Greg Jones, Andrés Rosberg, Laura Catena, Anabelle Sielecki, and Roberto de la Mota.

North American inspiration came from Fred Franzia, Joey Franzia, Kylor Williams, John Williams, Julie Johnson, Patrick Egan, Warren Winiarski, Jean-Charles Boisset, Jim Gordon, Jason Lett, Ted Baseler, Ernst Loosen, Bob Bertheau, David Rosenthal, Lynda Eller, Kirsten Elliott, and everyone at Chateau Ste. Michelle. And I cannot forget Howard Soon, Chuck and Tracy Reininger, Michael and Lauri Corliss, George Matelich, Randal and Jennifer Hopkins, Tom Hedges, Mike and Karen Wade, Robin Wade Hansen, Sumner Erdman, Charlie Hoppes, Eric McKibben, Jean-François-Pellet, Wade Wolfe, Gregg Alger, Jim Thomssen, Steve Rannekleiv, Tom Collins, John Aguirre, Gert and Mike Trbovich, Marty and Megan Clubb, Luca Paschina, Domenico Zonin. A thousand thanks to you all and a thousand apologies to everyone I have accidentally left off the list. Wine brings people together and I have been lucky to meet so many talented people who were willing to teach me a little of what they know.

This book did not make itself. I appreciate the expertise and support of the professionals at Rowman & Littlefield who have made it possible: editorial director Susan McEachern, production editor Jehanne Schweitzer, copyeditor Tom Holton, typesetter Wanda Ditch, and proofreader Beth Richards.

And finally the biggest thanks of all (and hugs and kisses, too) to my partner in crime and Wine Economist contributing editor, Sue Veseth.

Selected Bibliography

Here are a few of my favorite references from among the dozens that I consulted in writing this book (check the Endnotes section for a more complete collection). All these books are good enough to read!

Catena, Laura. *Vino Argentino: An Insider's Guide to the Wines and Wine Country of Argentina*. San Francisco: Chronicle Books, 2010.

D'Agata, Ian. *Native Wine Grapes of Italy*. Berkeley: University of California Press, 2014.

Fabrizio, Gianni, Eleonora Guerini, and Marco Sabellico (editors). *Italian Wines 2015*. New York: Gambero Rosso, 2014.

Fanet, Jacques (translated from the French by Florence Brutton). *Great Wine Terroirs*. Berkeley: University of California Press, 2004.

Gariglio, Giancarlo, and Fabio Giavedoni (editors). *Slow Wine Guide 2014*. Bra, Italy: Slow Food Editore, 2013.

Geddes, Robert. *Australian Wine Vintages 2014*. Adelaide, Australia: Geddes A Drink Publications, 2013.

Haeger, John Winthrop. *Riesling Rediscovered: Bold, Bright, and Dry*. Berkeley: University of California Press, 2016.

Hancock, David. *Oceans of Wine: Madeira and the Emergence of American Trade and Taste*. New Haven, CT: Yale University Press, 2009.

Heskett, Randall, and Joel Butler. *Divine Vintage: Following the Wine Trail from Genesis to the Modern Age.* New York: Palgrave Macmillan, 2012.

Hilton, James. *Lost Horizon.* New York: William Morrow, 1933.

James, Tim. *Wines of the New South Africa: Tradition and Revolution.* Berkeley: University of California Press, 2013.

Kladstrup, Don and Petie. *Wine and War: The French, the Nazis and the Battle for France's Greatest Treasure.* New York: Broadway Books, 2001.

Lofts, Graeme. *Heart and Soul: Australia's First Families of Wine.* Melbourne: John Wiley & Sons Australia, 2010.

Mount, Ian. *The Vineyard at the End of the World: Maverick Winemakers and the Rebirth of Malbec.* New York: Norton: 2011.

Mustacich, Suzanne. *Thirsty Dragon: China's Lust for Bordeaux and the Threat to the World's Best Wines.* New York: Henry Holt, 2015.

Page, Martin. *The First Global Village: How Portugal Changed the World.* Alfragide, Portugal: Casa das Letras, 2002.

Palin, Michael. *Around the World in 80 Days.* London: BBC Books, 1989.

Peterson, Richard G. *The Winemaker.* Loch Lomond, CA: Meadowlark Publishing, 2015.

Phillips, Rod. *French Wine: A History.* Berkeley: University of California Press, 2016.

Pigott, Stuart. *Best White Wine on Earth: The Riesling Story.* New York: Abrams, 2014.

Pinney, Thomas. *The Makers of American Wine.* Berkeley: University of California Press, 2012.

Pitte, Jean-Robert (English translation by M. B. DeBoise). *Bordeaux/Burgundy: A Vintage Rivalry.* Berkeley: University of California Press, 2008.

Platter, John and Erica. *Africa Uncorked: Travels in Extreme Wine Territory.* South San Francisco: Wine Appreciation Guild, 2002.

Robinson, Jancis, and Linda Murphy. *American Wine: The Ultimate Companion to the Wines and Wineries of the United States.* Berkeley: University of California Press, 2013.

Robinson, Jancis, Julia Harding, and José Vouillamoz. *Wine Grapes.* New York: HarperCollins Ecco, 2012.

Taber, George. *To Cork or Not to Cork.* New York: Scribner, 2007.

Theise, Terry. *Reading Between the Wines.* Berkeley: University of California Press, 2010.

Verne, Jules. *Around the World in Eighty Days.* New York: Sterling, 2008.

Index

About the Author

Mike Veseth is an authority on global wine markets who travels the world studying wine economics and speaking to wine industry groups. He reports his discoveries on his blog, The Wine Economist (WineEconomist.com), and in more than a dozen books including *Wine Wars, Extreme Wine*, and *Money, Taste, and Wine: It's Complicated!* Gourmand International recognized The Wine Economist as the "Best in the World" Wine Blog in 2015 and *Money, Taste, and Wine: It's Complicated!* received the award for "Best in the World" Wine Writing in 2016.

Mike is Professor Emeritus of International Political Economy at the University of Puget Sound, where he is a member of the board of trustees. He was honored as Washington State's Professor of the Year in 2010. He has a B.A. in Mathematics and Economics from the University of Puget Sound and an M.S. and Ph.D. in Economics from Purdue University. When Mike isn't circling the globe in search of new wine stories he lives in Tacoma, Washington, with his wife, Sue Veseth, and Mooch the Cat.